1974

ALSO BY FRANCINE PROSE

1974

A PERSONAL HISTORY

FRANCINE PROSE

HARPER

An Imprint of HarperCollins*Publishers*

HarperCollins books may be purchased for educational, business, or sales promotional use. For information, please email the Special Markets Department at SPsales@harpercollins.com.

FIRST EDITION

Designed by Elina Cohen

Library of Congress Cataloging-in-Publication Data has been applied for.

ISBN 978-0-06-331409-2

24 25 26 27 28 LBC 5 4 3 2 1

FOR HOWIE

That world! These days it's all been erased and they've rolled it up like a scroll and put it away somewhere. Yes, I can touch it with my fingers. But where is it?

—DENIS JOHNSON

In those days I would follow anyone who offered me so much as a sardine.

—SAINT TERESA OF ÁVILA

San Francisco, winter 1974. There was less traffic then. At ten on a weekday night, Tony could take his ten-year-old putty-colored Buick up to fifty-five and slam-bounce up and down the hills along Taylor Street.

Maybe Tony thought that someone was following him. He certainly thought so later. Maybe he was right all along. He kept checking his rearview mirror. He'd make sharp U-turns and veer into alleys. He had every reason to suspect that he was under surveillance, and he drove like someone trying to elude whoever was pursuing him.

He said that we were right to be afraid. He said that he was living proof of what could happen if you pissed off the wrong people. Actually, the *right* people: the government and the military, the criminals and the liars. He said they'd been working against us for years and that it would take courage and determination to defeat them. He said that if we told the truth, if we tried to talk about what happened, they called us paranoid.

That was more or less what I thought, and I liked hearing him say it.

I was always looking for things we had in common, maybe because on the surface we must have seemed so different. He was Southern. I'd grown up in New York. He was an aerospace engineer turned radical activist. I'd published a novel and was about to publish another. I was in my twenties. He was ten years older. I had long dark hair. He was bald with a shoulder-length fringe. I was at the beginning of my career as a writer, and he was beginning to think that his career was over.

We both cared about politics. We both liked stories. We both liked to laugh. We were both less easygoing than we tried to appear.

• • •

We often talked about books. It turned out that *Gravity's Rainbow* was one of our favorite novels. It spoke to our belief that history and the forces that shaped it were in every way more sinister than the most evil scenarios we could imagine.

In 1974, fans of Thomas Pynchon's dense, confusing seven-hundred-page conspiracy novel felt as if we'd found one another, recognized fellow . . . *what?* A group of people who distrusted groups. What did we take from the book? There is an order and a plan, but it's not the natural order, and it's certainly not God's plan. It's more likely the wicked scheme of Nazi war criminals operating an armaments and pharmaceutical conglomerate manufacturing Zyklon B gas and the V-2 rocket. That wasn't paranoia. That was just facing the facts.

Tony said we were right to worry. The impulse to destroy is as deep as the desire to create. When he was a kid in Virginia, he had a rogue history teacher who told his class that the reason humans are the only species that kills its own kind was because of some evil Egyptian poison in the apple that Eve gave Adam. Word got out, and the teacher was fired. Tony's science teacher told his students that wasn't true. He wasn't going to touch Adam and Eve, but he said that many animals are as bad or worse than humans when it comes to brutalizing their own kind. Lions, bears. Primates. Kangaroos. Meerkats.

I said, "Probably we're the only species that makes money from killing one another."

"Exactly," said Tony. "Precisely. That's our meerkat nature. So it will happen again. Stronger countries invading weaker countries, larger countries swallowing smaller ones, as long as there's a profit to be made, as long as it inflates some psycho dictator's ego. But we shouldn't be afraid. Because we are going to win. The war in Vietnam will end. Things are going to change."

"For the better," I said.

"For the better," said Tony.

It was a chilly, rainy winter, maybe no colder or wetter than any San Francisco winter, but it seemed that way to me. I had thought that California was warm year-round. The weather felt like a personal insult. I'd moved out West wearing flip-flops, and I refused to admit my mistake and buy a pair of shoes. My feet were always freezing. The heater in Tony's car barely functioned, and dampness seeped up through a hole in the floor. We rode with the windows shut. The car smelled like cigarette smoke, like the wet dog that neither of us had, like woolen coats in a grade school cloakroom. As we headed west through Outer Sunset and circling back along the avenues of Outer Richmond, bright streaks of neon signage dripped down the windshield onto the glistening streets.

I had no idea where we were going or where we would end up. I liked not knowing, not caring, not having to decide.

I was twenty-six. I liked feeling free, alive and on edge, even a little afraid. So what if my feet were cold? They wouldn't be cold forever.

I wanted to feel like an outlaw. So did everyone I knew. Bonnie and Clyde were our Romeo and Juliet. I still have a photograph of the leaders of the Barrow gang, the Depression-era bank-robber lovebirds. In heels and a long dark dress with a knitted top, Bonnie pokes a rifle and one finger into Clyde's chest, his immaculate white shirt. Slightly slumped, his hat pushed back, Clyde is looking at her, half amused, half besotted.

Played by Faye Dunaway and Warren Beatty in the 1967 film, the couple couldn't have been more beautiful or languidly stylish. They were our outlaw-lover superstars, hotter than Seberg and Belmondo. That Clyde was apparently impotent made their love all the more tragic, chaste and operatic. I can still see their mustard-colored 1934 Ford sedan death car bucking and jumping as the hail of bullets pierced it or bounced off.

I didn't want *that*, obviously. But I wanted the rush. I had just recovered from two bouts of what the early desert saints called the pain of the distance from God. The fogginess, the loneliness, the lack of direction or purpose. They called it spiritual aridity: the inability to be touched or consoled by prayer. Though I didn't believe in God, I understood what they meant. I was better now, or mostly. I wanted to stay that way.

I wanted to feel the thrill of not knowing or caring where I was going or what I was *supposed* to be doing. The dreamlike unreality of those high-speed drives was nerve-racking but weirdly relaxing. Nothing was expected of me. I didn't have to think. I hardly had to speak. All I had to do was listen.

From 1972 until 1975, I lived, for months at a time, in San Francisco. There was no reason for me to be in California, except that I liked it there, and because it was across a continent from Cambridge, Massachusetts, where I had left my husband and dropped out of school and never wanted to return. In those years, I often chose a place to live because it was as far as possible from the place I was escaping.

I'd stay in San Francisco through the fall and winter, then leave and go back to New York to see my family and friends, then return out West. I lived in the Inner Sunset district, not far from Buena Vista Park, in a sunny apartment with two roommates, a couple I'll call Henry and Grace.

California might have felt like a long vacation in limbo if I hadn't begun to think of myself as a writer. One perk of being a writer was that I could tell myself that I was working even when I wasn't. I liked to think I was becoming a person on whom, as Henry James said, nothing was wasted. It sounded right, but I wondered about following James's advice because he and I always felt so differently about the characters in his novels. Did he really want me to side with his hapless innocent marks when his amoral scoundrels were so much more charismatic?

I liked thinking that my job description was to watch and try to understand who people were, to intuit what they'd been through, what they revealed or tried to hide, what they said versus what they meant. The challenge was to find the right sentences, the right words, the right *punctuation* to get it down on the page.

Meanwhile I was at that stage when time and the body are signaling the unconscious: If you are going to make stupid mistakes, you should probably make them now. Everything seemed like a matter of life and death and simultaneously inconsequential. Everything broken could be fixed. Everything that was incomplete could be finished, or anyway, so I hoped.

I knew that my life and the world around me were changing, that something was ending and something else beginning, but I was too close—too inside of it—to have any idea what it was.

Four years after the last time I saw Tony, I had my first child, and from the moment my son was born, I was no longer the same person who thought it was *interesting* and *fun* to speed around San Francisco in the middle of the night with a stranger chain-smoking Camels, alternating stretches of silence with long bouts of storytelling and weeping.

Funny stories, not-funny stories, frightening stories, stories that veered and rambled, stories that might have been only partly true, and then the silent tears. Sometimes, when Tony cried, he shook his head, as if he couldn't believe he was crying. I stared ahead, out the windshield, partly to give him privacy but mostly to set a good example of keeping your eyes on the road.

Sometimes he'd tell stories with confusing chronologies or that lacked the smooth transitions that would have made them possible to follow. It often seemed as if words were moving through him, bubbling like drops from a fountain. He didn't seem to care about being admired or respected, and no matter how personally, even confessionally he was speaking, he maintained an air of privacy, an appealing reserve.

His highest term of praise was *moved.* When he talked about the most important moments in his life, he'd say, "I was very *moved.*"

Also he was a rebel. My friends and I liked bad boys: John

Lennon, Bob Dylan, the Rolling Stones. James Dean. The Crystals sang, *He's a rebel, and he'll never be any good.* When the waitress asks Brando, the hot biker in *The Wild One,* "What are you rebelling against, Johnny?" and he answers, "Whaddaya got?" his reply landed somewhere between a joke and a prescription for living. My friends and I wanted romance, which didn't necessarily mean seeking the most stable romantic partners with the most promising careers.

Tony had been a soldier without having to go to war. He had tried to stop a war. He'd tried to change something and lost everything, or almost everything, and that was attractive too: the wounded warrior who could still see the humor in his situation.

In December 1971, two years before I met Tony, he and Daniel Ellsberg were indicted, under the Espionage Act, for leaking information—a secret seven-thousand-page report known as the Pentagon Papers—that, according to the authorities, could jeopardize national security and endanger our soldiers in Southeast Asia. The two had met at the RAND Corporation, in Santa Monica, a think tank with close ties to the US military. Locating their headquarters out West, the company hoped to preserve some independence from Washington, though how much autonomy could they expect when they were funded by the government? The "Orwellian" (Tony's word) organization of analysts, strategists, and economists helped orchestrate the war in Vietnam.

Daniel Ellsberg and Tony Russo photocopied the documents that Ellsberg smuggled, in sections, from the RAND files. Commissioned by Defense Secretary Robert McNamara, the study proved that the executive branch of our government had been lying for decades to Congress and to the American people about our involvement in Vietnam.

We'd been told we were spreading democracy, preventing a communist takeover, supporting the Vietnamese in their fight for independence. But the Pentagon Papers—which were published, in part, in the *New York Times*, the *Washington Post*, and numerous other news outlets—proved that the United States started out to help the French keep control of colonial Vietnam. We'd stayed because money was being made building planes and bombs, and because five successive presidents didn't want to be the guy who got kicked out of Asia. The Pentagon Papers proved that millions had died and a country had been destroyed so that Lyndon B. Johnson and Richard M. Nixon wouldn't look like losers. The documents proved the so-called "quagmire theory"—the idea that we'd gone into Vietnam for honorable reasons and gotten stuck there without a viable exit strategy— was always a fiction devised to conceal the truth.

What was in the report that we hadn't known before? The "Gulf of Tonkin incident," the attack on an American ship that was used to justify our intercession in Vietnam, never happened. Bombing the North was accomplishing nothing except killing thousands of people, 80 percent of them civilians. The failure of the pacification program and the scorched-earth policy, the toxicity of Agent Orange—the government knew it all, and kept it secret. The Pentagon Papers confirmed what the antiwar movement had never been able to prove: Our presence in Vietnam was unwanted. We'd committed war crimes.

In 1974, Tony was still known, at least among activists, as an anti–Vietnam War whistleblower and free speech hero. By then, he had spent forty-seven days in jail for refusing to testify against Ellsberg or to appear before the grand jury unless the session was open to the public so he could use it to talk about why we were in Asia. His hope was that the publicity generated by the trial might reach people who were still unaware of what the Pentagon Papers had shown. Despite the growing evidence that the release of the Pentagon Papers wouldn't significantly alter the political landscape, Tony still believed, or tried to believe, that the truths they revealed and the lies they exposed would blow the country apart.

That was the winter when Patty Hearst was kidnapped from the Berkeley apartment where she lived with her graduate student boyfriend, the former math teacher at her high school. That was the winter when she was held captive by the Symbionese Liberation Army, which demanded, in exchange for her release, two million dollars' worth of free food be distributed to the poor. That was the winter when the food giveaway in West Oakland degenerated into a riot. That was the winter when the SLA decided to hold on to their captive princess until they figured out what to do next.

The April 15 bank robbery that turned Patty Hearst into a gun-slinging, fuzzed-out poster girl happened at the Hibernia Bank branch very near our apartment. The house where she would be arrested was also nearby. My roommates and I knew about the robbery but not yet about the safe house.

The story about the kidnapped heiress and the cult led by a formerly incarcerated Black man—Donald DeFreeze, now code-named Field Marshal Cinque—was media gold. A white-girl disappearance (always newsworthy) was spun as a conclusive I-told-you-so about the hippies, radicals, and Black activists who had tried to make America feel guilty about racism, inequality, and the war. Thanks to what we heard about Field Marshal Cinque, the world was finally being shown that the self-styled revolutionaries were thugs, abducting an innocent white girl for the "crime" of being rich, throwing her in a closet, demanding a ridiculous ransom: If her family wanted her back, they had to feed every poor person in California!

With its irresistible mix of tabloid gossip and political paranoia, the story stayed in the news: the innocent billionaire brainwashed by radical maniacs who taught her to call her media-empire family "fascist insects" and "pig Hearsts." Code-named Tania, Patty took a new lover, code-named Cujo. The photo of Tania in a beret, holding an automatic weapon in front of the black-and-red SLA flag emblazoned with its insignia, a many-headed serpent, became the parent-approved sex poster for the radical teenager's bedroom.

Grace and Henry advised me not to mention Patty Hearst to their friend Tony Russo, who was coming over to play poker. I appreciated the warning. The abduction was very much in the news. Strangers chatted about it in line at the supermarket.

Apparently Henry had made an offhand remark about the kidnapping, and Tony said, with real venom, "I don't want to hear another word of that bullshit." It was puzzling because normally, Grace said, Tony was so good-natured and polite. It turned out that Tony believed that our neighborhood was crawling with FBI agents searching for Patty Hearst. When they found her or quit looking for her, they would go back to following and harassing him, if they'd ever stopped.

Grace and Henry told me that Tony was having a hard time. As far as they knew, he was unemployed. He'd been doing community outreach and civil rights organizing in Los Angeles, where he'd worked for the Los Angeles County Probation Department. But he'd lost his job there after he'd gone to prison. No one understood why he'd moved to San Francisco, nor how he paid the rent. Henry said the Black Panthers had raised money for Tony's legal team, and that his young, pretty, radical ex-wife sold sandwiches in the courthouse lobby, during the trial, to dramatize his need for help paying his lawyers.

I recognized Tony immediately. I had seen him in newspaper photos and on TV, surrounded by journalists. He always stood just behind Daniel Ellsberg's shoulder, waiting his turn at the mike. I'd noticed him partly because, in his butcher boy cap, shaggy sideburns, rumpled jacket and tie, he looked so unlike Ellsberg in his elegant suit and good haircut. I'd noticed Tony partly because he always seemed so calm and contained, even a little amused, while the frenetic reporters shouted questions and thrust their microphones in his face.

When Henry introduced us, Tony looked at me a beat too long, maintaining a thin but acceptable margin between friendliness and appraisal. By 1974, most of the men I knew had learned better than to look at women that way.

I wanted him to notice me. He was a famous antiwar hero. He'd done what we all should have done. He'd lived the way we all should have lived, suffered as we might have suffered if things had gone as badly for us as they had for him. I wanted to think that I would have had the courage to do what he did, to help leak a secret report about Vietnam that my work-friend happened to be lugging around in his briefcase. To go to jail, if necessary.

Tony said, "It's a pleasure to meet you."

He had a Southern accent and a low musical voice. His voice and his delivery were among his most attractive qualities. He wasn't conventionally handsome, but he was *interesting-looking*. He had the slightly pudgy, appealing face of a good-tempered hypermasculine baby. He chain-smoked unfiltered cigarettes and didn't look entirely healthy, yet there was something radiant about him: the inner light of a zealot. His metal-framed eyeglasses glittered. He was soft-spoken, quick-witted, and extremely smart.

Later, when I read Leigh Hunt's description of John Keats, I thought of Tony, his energy and sensibility, his upper lip, his tears: "He was under the middle height . . . his shoulders were very broad for his size; he had a face in which energy and sensibility were remarkably mixed up . . . Every feature was at once strongly cut and delicately alive. If there was any faulty expression it was in the mouth which was not without something of a character of pugnacity . . . the upper lip projected a little over the under . . . At the recital of a beautiful action or noble thought [his eyes] would suffuse with tears."

Tony was very funny, though when you say that about a person, you can't think of one funny thing they said, just as you can describe someone as charming without being able to begin to explain what charm is, exactly.

The poker games at Henry and Grace's were penny-ante, in no way serious, and the games got less and less serious as the players smoked more and more weed. No one cared about winning or losing. The whole point, for Henry and Grace, was using the stylish vintage wooden wheel that spun on casters and held slotted stacks of Bakelite poker chips. They'd bought it at a yard sale.

I watched Tony as I shuffled and dealt, put down and picked up the cards. I looked at him until he looked back. I could tell that he noticed, that the famous antiwar hero was watching me too, and that his focus wasn't that of a player trying to psych out an opponent's hand.

Tony mentioned, in passing, that he and his coworkers in Saigon had played a lot of poker. After that he was silent for a long time. At one point he said that there were two different types of experience, two different kinds of knowledge. Both had to do with time. The first kind of knowledge comes back, even after a long lapse, like riding a bicycle. The second kind was use it or lose it. Forget and you never remember. He said that poker was an experience of the second kind. By then, we'd smoked quite a lot of weed. It didn't matter that no one understood what he meant.

When he spoke, he was speaking to me. Henry and Grace noticed too. At some point it became clear, without anything having been said, that I would be going home with Tony when he left.

Tony wasn't a great poker player, or so it seemed. I wondered if he was losing to me on purpose, which was flattering in one way and not in another.

Henry and Grace must have told him that my first book had done well—well, that is, for a literary debut novel published in 1973, which meant that it got good reviews and was perceived as a success. My second novel was coming out, and I was (supposedly) working on a third.

During a break from the game, Tony congratulated me on my book, and on the forthcoming one. He told me that he thought my being a novelist was amazing. Maybe that was true, or partly true. But it was also the kind of thing that men had recently learned to say if they wanted to get laid.

Also, in an amazing coincidence, he too was writing a book. He'd come to San Francisco to work on it, because it was less distracting here than in LA, where the postal deliverers and the trash collectors were still losing his letters and strewing his garbage around the alley behind his house. It was disturbing, not just because it made life harder, but because he'd imagined that those guys would be on his side. They and their sons were the ones being sent off to fight in the war that Tony had tried to end.

All that time he'd studied engineering and government, he said, he'd dreamed of becoming a writer. He said, "I wrote all the time in jail, when I could, until the guards took my journal away, and then beat me up for objecting. After that I wrote in my head. Maybe you could take a look at some of the stuff I'm writing. Just a couple of pages. It's not really . . . literary. I'm not aiming to write a masterpiece. I'm just trying to get it down, what happened in Vietnam, what I saw there . . ."

I didn't know what to say. It occurred to me that we'd started off talking about me and ended by talking about Tony. I was just starting out as a writer. I had no idea what I was doing, no more or less than I ever had, no more or less than I do now. I had no advice to give, but already people were asking me to read their novels. I tried to find excuses that wouldn't hurt anyone's feelings.

And yet I was flattered that Tony wanted me to read his book. That a hero was asking for my help meant there was something I could do, that there was a way I could contribute to the work for which Tony had sacrificed so much. I could show him how to line-edit if he thought it might be useful. I wondered if the invitation to look at his writing was code-speak for sex, but I couldn't tell with Tony, and for the moment it didn't matter.

High, I played a tighter and more focused game, even as my friends' attention drifted. I wasn't a great poker player, but neither did I need the order of the hands written out for me or the rules of the specialty games explained. I depended more on luck than players who knew what they were doing. That night I drew some unpromising hands, but I thought ahead and watched and won. I took it as a sign that I was doing something right—and that it was a good idea to leave with Tony when the evening ended. As far as I knew, neither of us had romantic commitments that would complicate things.

We settled our debts. Tony had lost thirty dollars, twenty of them to me. For some reason this seemed funny and like a secret between us. How could *that* have been secret? Our friends were right there, stacking the poker chips. Nor was it a secret that Tony and I were leaving together.

When Tony's back was turned, Grace shook her head at me and mouthed *Don't!*, a twitch of warning that only I saw and that I pretended not to notice.

Tony and I got our coats. We both wore black leather jackets, another thing that seemed funny. Tony helped me into mine. My arms missed the sleeves, which caused a bit of awkward flailing around. We laughed and tried again.

"Button up," Tony said. "Or is it zip up?" He looked at my jacket. "I was right the first time."

I said, "San Francisco is always colder than I expected."

"Tell me about it," said Tony. "I can't get used to it."

That was how we established that neither of us was from there, nor did we plan to stay.

He asked if I minded riding around in the car for a while.

I said I liked it, which was true. Riding around a city, any city, has always been one of my favorite things to do. I loved seeing San Francisco through the window of a moving car. I had never stopped being thrilled by how you could turn a corner and a slice of the blue Pacific might flash up like a dolphin. I loved the wooden housefronts faded salmon gray by the weather. I loved how the city's residents took civic pride in the days when fog enveloped the neighborhoods like a giant furry cocoon.

• • •

All during the card game Tony had been wry, low-key, and amused, but now, with just the two of us in the car, he seemed tense and preoccupied. As he sped off toward Judah Street, his glance kept tracking toward the rearview mirror.

After a while he turned on the radio to the same station Henry and Grace listened to in their cars. The Chi-Lites, the Delfonics, the O'Jays, the Stylistics, Harold Melvin and the Blue Notes. I was pleased and relieved. Music meant a lot—maybe too much—to me. In college, I'd been lonely because none of the people I met during my first weeks had ever heard of James Brown. I'd slept with guys just because they liked the same songs I did.

I liked it that the station Tony had on played the so-called Philadelphia sound. *If loving you is wrong, I don't want to be right. Didn't I blow your mind this time? You, you make me feel brand-new. Me and Mrs. Jones, we got a thing goin' on.* So many of the songs were about hopeless, passionate, adulterous sex, about the love you could die for, die *from*, the love that keeps reminding you that you will never understand it. It's the kind of music that makes you wish you were in love, the kind that makes you long to fall in love.

I told myself, Don't. Seriously, don't. Don't let the music touch you. I'd read somewhere that love comes in through the eyes, so I tried not to look too directly at Tony. It was easy, sitting side by side in the car. The Buick had no console between us, so we could have sat very close. We could have touched. But we didn't.

"*If you don't know me by now, you will never, never, never know me,*" Tony sang along. Prophetically, as it turned out.

He hit all the falsetto notes.

"You can sing," I said.

"Once a choir boy, always a choir boy," he said.

Eventually Tony turned off the radio, and then it was just silence and the protests of an old car being pushed too hard. He hit the gas and drove the avenues fast, without speaking, out through the Sunset, then across the park and back through the Outer Richmond, without speaking, then around and out Parnassus, without speaking, past Henry and Grace's apartment. When we passed their house for the third time, my roommates' bedroom light was out, and only then did I realize how late it was.

He said, "I know it's not a great idea to just drive for the hell of it. I know about the gas crisis. I know that the so-called crisis is the usual bullshit designed to make more money for OPEC. The gas isn't going to run out. It's just going to get more expensive. In case you're wondering, I have two license plates, one with an odd number, one with an even, so I can fill up wherever I want. I just have to remember not to go to the same gas station two days in a row."

"How did you get two license plates?" I asked.

"That's classified information." Tony waited a beat, then laughed.

I'd assumed that we would be going to Tony's apartment. But it was becoming clear that we weren't, at least not yet. I didn't care. Whatever happened was fine. It wasn't as if I was in the grip of crazy lust or as if I imagined that Tony was going to be the love of my life.

I suppose I already had the kind of crush on him that can begin when you want to be the focus of someone's attention, and then you are. Especially when you are young and that person is important or famous. Not only was Tony a hero, an antiwar celebrity, but he had said all the right things that night, hit the right marks about my being a writer. I still believed that you could *decide* to let love happen or not.

I had just escaped a marriage that had been a mistake. The last thing I wanted was a "relationship." I couldn't think of the word without imagining it between ironic quotes. I couldn't picture myself settling down and having children, though that was precisely what I would do four years later.

I didn't want a serious love, certainly not with Tony. From the beginning I sensed that something about him was . . . the word I decided on was *troubled*. Everyone has troubles. Certainly I had. An aura of unease surrounded him, the faint distressing buzz of an electrical panel with a burnt fuse and some wires pulled loose. I didn't want to adopt his demons or share his resentments and regrets. What did Nelson Algren say? Never eat at a place called Mom's. Never play cards with a guy named Doc. Never sleep with someone (he said "a woman") who has more problems than you do.

Of course life is never as simple as Algren's wise-guy rules of avoidance. Tony was charismatic. He was brave. He'd been to Vietnam. He'd interviewed prisoners, peasants, scooter drivers. He'd seen the horrors of war. He'd help steal the Pentagon Papers. He'd gone to jail. And now he wanted me to listen, to hear what he had been through. He seemed to think I could help. He'd come to San Francisco to write a book, and I was a writer.

Neon signs flashed past. A Russian restaurant, a laundromat, a motel, a massage parlor. Brightly colored letters wobbled in the mist. I was still pretty high. I liked everything I saw. I liked it that Tony didn't care about anything scenic or touristic: views of the Golden Gate Bridge, Chinatown, Lombard Street. Nothing like that. All that mattered was speed and minimal traffic, hitting the waves of green lights and running the red

ones. If Tony stopped, it was only to open a new pack of cigarettes.

I wasn't required to admire anything. I didn't have to say,
How beautiful! I didn't have to speak. What I wanted to say was,
Watch out! You're going to kill someone! But I didn't say that
either.

I was too busy paying attention, trying to focus on what
Tony was telling me. To remember it word for word. Not to
write about it. Not then. But because it seemed important.

I held onto the edge of my seat as the car hit a pothole, levi-
tated, and slammed down on the blacktop. Neither of us spoke,
but I felt as if we were chattering wordlessly into the silence.

It had begun to drizzle. The light from the streetlamps
striped the windshield. I imagined the light bar on the Xerox
machine on which Tony and Ellsberg copied the Pentagon Papers, the glowing tube swinging back and forth, back and forth.
The work must have been tedious, but that's how copies were
made then. Page by page. Slap the paper down on the glass,
lower the flap, wait for the light to make its double turn, lift the
flap, remove the page, repeat twenty-one thousand times. Forty-
seven thick bound volumes. The equivalent of *Moby-Dick* single-
spaced on typing paper and stacked up fourteen times over.

I said, "Copying all those pages must have been like a fairy
tale, like something Rumpelstiltskin makes you do so he won't
steal your baby. How much time did it take, how much paper,
how many ink cartridges did you go through, how many machines broke down? Copy machines are temperamental. They
break all the time. They—"

I made myself stop. I sounded like a girl I knew in college
whose social anxiety made her go on and on about her uncle's
dachshund's hip dysplasia. What could be more *boring* than
talking about copy machines?

Tony turned toward me and smiled a slow Cheshire Cat grin. He'd smiled like that at the poker game, when I'd bluffed and won. But he hadn't smiled since we'd been in the car.

He said, "If it's okay with you, I am really really *really* tired of talking about Xerox machines." The smile was to reassure me that he didn't mean to hurt my feelings.

"I'm sorry," I said.

"Please don't be sorry," he said. "Asking about the Xeroxing is the first thing everyone does."

I didn't want him to see me as the kind of person who did the first thing that everyone does, but I'd already done it. He drove in silence until he pulled up to a curb and stopped. I'd lost track of where we were. It was too dark to see.

We got out. I heard the ocean. The air was soggy, and the rain had sharpened into cold, spiky needles. I chafed my arms. It occurred to me that Tony hadn't touched me all evening, not once, not even brushing my fingers by accident as we'd dealt and picked up our cards.

We stood on the edge of a drop-off. There was just enough moonlight filtering through the clouds to see the dark stone pools below us, the cracked basins full of muck. Beyond the ruins were the beach and fog and the black waves rolling in.

The clouds broke, and the moon floated in one of the stone pools like a huge soggy Communion wafer.

"Do you know where we are?" he said.

"The Sutro Baths," I said.

"Good one," Tony said.

In 1896, Adolph Sutro, a developer-entrepreneur, built a combination aquarium, amusement pavilion, and public bathhouse, a turn-of-the-century water park with seven pools and room for ten thousand guests. It was doomed by the Great Depression. The land was slated for redevelopment; then the baths burned down, and it remained in ruins. You could walk on the walls, and around the pools, or look down at it from above.

A damp wind blew in from the sea. Tony took off his jacket and draped it across my shoulders. It was uncomfortable, wearing one leather jacket over another, but it made me feel taken care of, and the salt mist brought tears to my eyes.

Everyone knows that when you're attracted to someone, the discovery of a shared passion can seem like proof that you're meant to be together. You like the full moon? Amazing! I like the full moon too! You like beer? Me too! Friendships can take a similar leap. Maybe we just love the voice—the whisper—telling us that we're not alone.

Henry and Grace had introduced me to the Sutro Baths. It was tricky to reach by public transportation, and it was off the standard San Francisco tourist itinerary, so hardly anyone went there. Not everybody saw the magic in a string of swampy pools at the edge of the ocean. But when friends visited from the East, I told them to go.

I loved the Sutro Baths: their beauty, their desolation, their mystery. So did Tony, it seemed.

We stood on a rise above the pools, watching shafts of moonlight sweep across the crumbling walls as clouds drifted across the night sky. The baths were how I imagined Pompeii or Hadrian's Villa.

Tony said, "It's like every ruin. Somebody's empire didn't work out. Or it did until it didn't."

We fell silent. The only sound was the slap of the waves. There was no one else around. We stood there—close but not touching—on the edge of a cliff, in the dead of night.

Looking back, I'm a little frightened for that girl hanging out with a semi-famous, possibly unbalanced friend of a friend, looking down into a stone pool into which a person could be thrown and no one would ever find them.

But I wasn't scared then. Tony was one of the good guys. I knew he'd had a rough few years. Anyone would be rattled. It seemed *interesting* to be driven out there to hover above an abyss.

Maybe I was a little afraid. My family and friends were very far away. Were they even thinking of me? Henry and Grace knew who I'd left the house with, but not where we'd gone.

Tony wasn't going to hurt me.

A year ago I'd sat on a ledge, halfway up a Mayan pyramid, in Palenque. I didn't want to think about that now. I didn't want to wish I was there.

Tony said, "There were these magnificent fourth-century Hindu temples in central Vietnam that we will never see because we bombed them into baby powder on some bullshit tip-off that the so-called Viet Cong were sheltering there. You know what a US Army colonel told me? He said, 'The problem with those temples is that Ho Chi Minh is stewing his fucking disgusting chicken feet in the inner sanctum.'"

I laughed the isn't-that-horrible laugh that isn't a real laugh. It was strange that he'd mentioned Hindu temples because I'd been thinking not just about Pompeii but also about how the Sutro Baths reminded me of the ruins at Sarnath, where the Buddha preached his first sermon. I had been there a few years before, in what seemed like another life.

What was Tony saying? For an instant I'd thought of Sarnath and forgotten him and lost track.

He said, "Have you ever seen Rossellini's *Voyage to Italy*?"

There was just enough moonlight for him to see me shake my head no.

"The best bad-marriage film ever. Ingrid Bergman and George Sanders spend the movie ripping each other apart. He's a stuffy Brit ice cube, and she's whiny and bitchy, but pretty, there's that. Here's why I mention it. The ruins.

"He finally tells her, That's it. They're getting a divorce. But just then their Italian archeologist friend shows up to take them to Pompeii. They meet up with an excavation team, and bingo, the archeologists unearth a perfectly preserved man and a woman. Maybe the couple died together. Maybe they were husband and wife.

"Ingrid Bergman is practically in tears, but Sanders is still his chilly-old-bastard self. Soon they're walking down Main Street Pompeii, fighting about some marital bullshit. Look around, you upper-middle-class white Continental shitheads! You're stumbling through a ruined world, the apocalypse is over, the planet has been destroyed, and you're squabbling about *your marriage?*"

I hadn't said that the Sutro Baths were how I imagined Pompeii. How did Tony know? Perhaps it didn't require a giant leap of the imagination. Another sign of attraction: thinking the person can read your mind.

Tony picked up a stone and threw it down the hill. It bounced off the walls of the pool and dropped into the water. Plink, plink, plop. The soundtrack of a horror film just before the scream.

He said, "Look at you. You're shivering."

Only now did I notice how cold I was: My feet had never been so numb.

We got back in the car. Tony turned up the heater, which blew some cold air around, then quit.

He said, "Is it okay with you if we park here for a while?"

"Sure. What happens to them?" Self-consciousness made my voice crack.

"What happens to whom?"

"The couple in the film."

"Oh, right. They get stuck in a religious procession in Naples or somewhere. The mob comes barreling down the street. It's too packed for them to move the car, so they ditch it. They leave it there! She runs off and gets swept away by the crowd until he wades into the stampede and saves her. Long clinch. Passionate embrace. The crowd divides around them. They decide to stay together."

"Good luck to them," I said.

"Exactly. Marriage is the stupidest way the state has come up with for controlling our lives."

"You were married, right?"

"For about five minutes." He laughed. "It was her idea. She was pretty and young and smart, and she seemed to be up for everything, but I was misled. She's very radical, supposedly, but really she wanted to party with liberal Hollywood stars. She's since become a follower of the thirteen-year-old guru. Sometimes I wonder if she was an undercover FBI plant. In which case she should get a medal for distinguished service above and beyond the call of duty. You know why I thought she might be an agent? Her first and last names were the first and last names of a woman in a Hemingway novel. Some Yale English graduate FBI asshole's idea of a joke."

"Did you really think she was working for the FBI?"

"Everybody might be." He shrugged. "What can never be quantified is how much human interaction is a con, by which

I mean, excuse me, a circle jerk at the highest level. You bring your embryonic self to a person or a group, and if you are a certain kind of individual, maybe you have a gene for it, let's call it the Silly Putty gene, you're changed from a lump of Play-Doh—first into a living organism and then into something carved out of granite. A walking, talking tombstone."

I had no idea what he was saying, but I couldn't admit it.

"I don't think I have it," I said. "The Silly Putty gene."

"Me neither. So . . . where was I? Right. Psyops is the creation of a false front so no one can figure out who you are. We think that a person is our double, our soulmate, our cosmic twin, our best friend, whatever. That person wants to go for it, change the world, just like we do. But what that person really wants is to spend the summer on Martha's Vineyard."

Did he mean his ex-wife or Daniel Ellsberg or human beings in general?

I said, "I was married too. Also for about five minutes." Why had I said that? My marriage had lasted three years, from my final semester at college through two years of graduate school and a year of travel. "Nothing about it was that dramatic. I'm pretty sure my husband wasn't working for the FBI."

"You don't know," Tony said. "You never know who has a secret life and who doesn't."

I wasn't going to argue. My husband was not an FBI agent. He was a graduate student in chemistry. I had no idea what he was studying. He'd given up trying to explain it to me. My inability to understand his work was one of the many things about me that had begun to bore him. The only thing that didn't bore him was the affair he was having with one or maybe both of the women who lived upstairs from us in Cambridge. No one talked about open marriages. It would have seemed bourgeois and pervy. The sexual revolution meant that you were supposed to do what you wanted.

Tony pulled out of the parking spot and headed toward the Embarcadero. I was expecting another long silence when he said, "In the garden of one of those temples there was a six-foot stone dick sticking straight up out of the ground. We'll never see it now. It's gone. Bombed out of existence."

He laughed, and then he was crying. It was the first time I'd seen him cry. He wept silently, staring ahead. I didn't look at him, but I felt the air move, the way tears can change the atmosphere. When he turned toward me, his face was wet. He shrugged and smiled.

He said, "I don't want you thinking I'm the kind of guy who weeps over a six-foot granite hard-on. It's just that it's all so sad."

The pathetic fallacy: The sky was crying too. Within moments the rain intensified until it was almost car wash heavy.

"You need to turn on the window wipers," I said. "Really, Tony. You need to do it now."

"So I do," said Tony. "Thank you, ma'am. Everyone needs a copilot." He switched on the wipers.

I didn't like how much it pleased me when he'd called me his copilot. The last of the weed was wearing off, and my blood sugar was dropping.

"Are you hungry?" He got points for sensing it. Points for knowing I was there. For asking.

Minus points for not waiting for me to answer.

"Me too," he said. "I'm starving."

I wonder how Edward Hopper's paintings look to people too young to realize how realistic, how representative they are, how much like scenes and places that I can still remember: sad diners and all-night coffee shops with bad lighting and hardly anyone there. As far as I know, Hopper never painted a cafeteria. Maybe it was too hard. All those people in all that space and each one as alone as the solitary customer at the diner counter.

Tony's favorite place to eat was . . . let's call it the Martha Washington. I had been there before, with Henry and Grace. It was in the Tenderloin, not far from Compton's Cafeteria, where the drag queens hung out, and where there was an anti-police-harassment riot years before Stonewall. Compton's was like an aviary, alive with birdsong and bright plumage, but the Martha Washington was Dickensian, like a Lyons Corner House, one of those bleak steamy British tearooms smelling of ancient radiators, pipe smoke, and greasy toasted cheese.

The Martha Washington's major draw was the balance it maintained between privacy and community. Its large echoing space was more like a railroad station than a restaurant, and you could nurse a cup of coffee all night without anyone bothering you. No one was there to make friends. Its clientele included the homeless and semi-homeless, though homelessness then was nowhere near the catastrophe that it has since become in San Francisco. On the wall were Depression-era price lists that no one had bothered to take down.

The Martha Washington clientele included the overindulged coming down from drunks and highs, and people who looked as if they'd recently been kicked out of their houses. The sex workers might have livened up the mood, but they went to Compton's.

No one talked to anyone else, except a few sleepy taxi drivers exchanging traffic warnings and road-construction gossip.

The place also attracted slumming artists and writers who came to soak up the heady atmosphere of a room full of people at the end of their ropes. The Martha Washington was legendary. At first I thought that Tony wanted to show me that he knew a cool place, a giant dive bar that didn't serve alcohol but turned a blind eye when customers brought their own in paper bags.

The truth was that Tony liked it. He went there often. He knew where the condiments and restrooms were and how to navigate the space without making eye contact with another human being. I think he appreciated how alone you could be with lots of other people around you.

I'd nodded when he'd asked if I was hungry, but I wasn't, not really. I'd had dinner before the poker game. I wanted coffee with lots of sugar. It occurred to me that Tony wasn't sleeping, and that I was going to have to stay awake with him.

Now the not-sleeping might have suggested something wrong. Now that we're all amateur diagnosticians, we know that insomnia can be a symptom of a more serious condition. I wondered if Tony was on speed. But I didn't think so. I'd been with him all evening. Also he'd come to the cafeteria to eat, and speed was an appetite suppressant.

Tony said, "I guess one tray will do." I shuffled behind him along the food line. He knew the servers. They smiled and said hi. He ordered a plate of breakfast sausage, no eggs, no toast, thanks, just the sausage, and helped himself to a thick slice of gluey blueberry pie. I filled a cup with coffee, poured in some cream, and grabbed a handful of sugars.

The woman who rang us up said, "I'll have to charge you for all those sugars." Only when she saw the sausage and blueberry pie did she look up from the register. She said, "Oh, it's you! How are you keeping, honey?" The warmth of her greeting seemed like evidence of Tony's good character.

"Fine, thank you. And you?"

"Keeping on keeping on," she said. She looked at me. She must have wondered who would hang out with a guy who survived on breakfast sausage and blueberry pie. She must have wondered who would let him live that way.

She said, "You need to get Tony to eat some vegetables."

I laughed. "I'll try."

"Good luck with that," said Tony.

We sat as far as possible from anyone else. Tony cut the sausage in bits and mashed it together with the pie. I tried not to stare at the doughy purple mound studded with bits of greasy chopped meat. I had never seen an adult play with his food like that or eat something so unhealthy and disgusting. Or anyway not since grade school lunchroom, which made it kind of touching. Trying to see the child in the grown-up was one way to get to know a person. I could imagine Tony as a middle school math genius, the overcompensating class clown trying to make the others laugh with the unappetizing concoctions he ate. The boy I pictured had Tony's round, balding head.

He said, "Want a taste? It's delicious."

"No thanks," I said. "I'm fine."

He said, "I had a friend at RAND. Tom Chan. Those racist fuckwads had a rule against ordering in Chinese food for lunch. Those pigs suspected the scallion pancakes were laced with bubonic plague. No one was serving ethnic lunch in the company cafeteria. Not even tacos, not even chicken chow mein with canned noodles, which everybody ate back then. You can probably get that here if you want it." He gestured at the food line. "Should we find out?"

"That's all right," I said. "I'm fine." I was remembering how much Chinese takeout I'd eaten during that dark year in Cambridge, but I knew better than to lead with the bad habits I hoped to have left behind.

Tony said, "Tom used to mix sausage and berry pie. He said it tasted Cantonese. Like something his mom would make. He said, Try it. I did. I got to like it. Now it reminds me of him."

I said, "Is your friend dead?"

"How did you know?"

I didn't know how I knew or why I'd said that. "I heard something in your voice. Some . . . something."

Tony said, "Tom was killed in Vietnam. You'd make a good interrogator. Or maybe you're a witch."

I didn't answer because I didn't know if he meant any of that as a compliment. I finished my coffee. It tasted like scalded metal, but the sugary sludge at the bottom was delicious.

Tony cleaned his plate.

I was a little scared of the women's room, but I needed to pee. Sometimes the fears that had plagued me in Cambridge reappeared, like an eyelid twitch or a song I couldn't get out of my head. I wanted them to stay away, and so far they had. The proof was that I was with Tony at the Martha Washington Cafeteria, in the Tenderloin, in the middle of the night.

I made my way through the echoing vault of a room, past customers staring into space or animatedly conversing with themselves.

In the ladies' room, two guys were having sex in the stall next to mine. I found their happiness comforting, though it took me a while to pee.

When I got back to our table, Tony was standing up, waiting for me, smiling as if he was glad to see me and also relieved, as if he'd been afraid that I'd sneaked out a back door and left, or as if he'd been worried that he might have forgotten me and gone home without me. He'd remembered to wait.

We got back in the car, which, strangely enough, had begun to feel familiar. Safe, except for the speed at which Tony drove out toward the avenues.

When we left Henry and Grace's, I'd assumed that we would wind up at his apartment, but now I wasn't sure. I didn't know how I felt about that. Whatever happened seemed fine as long as we didn't injure ourselves or anyone else.

Tony said that there was such a thing as a green wave. It was like surfing. You hit the wave and you never got a red light. He said that was what it meant to be in tune with the universe. He told me that he had said that to Timothy Leary, but Leary thought he was joking or that Tony was as high as Leary was.

"Which I wasn't. Maybe Leary thought I wasn't famous or female or young and hot enough to be worth talking to."

"Where did you meet Leary?" I asked.

"At an antiwar rally. This was when they were still letting me appear in public during daylight hours. When they were still letting me talk."

I didn't ask who *they* were. The federal government? The FBI? The state of California? Daniel Ellsberg and his advisers?

After a while Tony said, "It was strange, looking in the mirror and thinking how many people wanted me to keep my mouth shut. There were a million things that RAND didn't want me to say."

He wanted me to ask, Like what? But I didn't. I wondered how many secrets Tony would have to tell me before I too was checking the rearview mirror. I liked the idea, and I didn't.

I was reaching the point where I preferred the peace I needed to write, or not write; preferred it to being an outlaw on the run; preferred it to living the high romance of Bonnie and Clyde, of

Patty Hearst. Of Tony Russo and Daniel Ellsberg. I didn't have to do this again. But I wanted to see what would happen.

"Here's a statistic they didn't like. Thirty-eight percent of the Vietnamese people I interviewed had lost children in the war. That number really ticked off my bosses. They did not want to hear that!" Tony said that last sentence so loud I flinched.

"Sorry," he said. "It still gets me. Those beautiful friendly kids. We'd drive into a town, and they'd surround us and say 'A-okay' and 'My pen is green,' random crumbs of English they'd picked up in school. They were so happy to see us. Like we were the circus come to town. I'd think of them in their classrooms, at their little desks, repeating, 'My pen is green, my pen is green,' and meanwhile the planes are circling, buzzing closer and closer, the bombs are falling until one of them finds the kids. Oops, sorry, we hit a school! And I was working for the experts who believed that we weren't bombing *enough*. No matter what I said or wrote, that was what we told Washington."

The silence got thicker. Tony drove along California toward the Presidio. I heard sirens, other cars, voices, but it all sounded blurry, as if we were slipping under water. Maybe the weed *hadn't* worn off completely. Who was this guy? Where was he taking me? I either had to say something or jump out at the next red light. I was still a little high, and now not in a good way.

What were my parents doing? They had no idea where I was. What would they think if they knew I was riding around with a guy who drove as if he was being followed and quite possibly was. My mother and father had wanted a safe, orderly life for me. A husband and a house. A damask tablecloth and fine china.

I said, "Didn't I read that Ellsberg got his kids to help with the photocopying? I heard that he let his son do some of the

Xeroxing and that he had his little daughter cutting the words "Top Secret" off the top of the sheets. And his ex-wife was furious at him for involving the kids in a federal crime."

Tony was silent as I went on. "And wasn't it the ex-wife or one of her relatives who ratted you out to the FBI?"

I was sorry as soon as I said it. I felt as if he was moving away, though he hadn't moved. This was worse than blithering about Xerox machines. I sounded stupid and shallow, diminishing the dangers Tony had faced, reducing his heroic ideals and hopes and ambitions to gossip about his friend's divorce.

"That's sort of what Dan said. He had his reasons. But I was never sure that his ex-mother-in-law was the one. It could have been anyone. I mean, hey, it could have been you."

"It wasn't me. I didn't know you then." I heard how clumsily that landed. I didn't know what else to say. I giggled. Humiliating!

"I'm joking," Tony said. "Obviously. Actually, there was a jealous reporter, a so-called colleague. He talked about us on the air. He named names. Our names. Those are the people you have to watch out for. The friends who wish they'd had the balls to do what you did." Tony's voice had gone tinny and flat, stripped of its warm Southern lilt.

He made a U-turn, drove for a while, then took another series of quick turns. After a while I realized that we were back on Parnassus Avenue. He pulled over in front of my apartment.

He said, "It's been a long night. I'm sorry, really I am. I need to get some rest. I haven't been sleeping all that well."

"Don't apologize," I said. I was exhausted. Sleeping in my own bed seemed like bliss. And there had been moments when Tony had unnerved me. I needed time to think. Even so, I felt dimly insulted. He must have known that I was willing to go home with him, and he'd decided against it. Decided against *me*.

Why was it *his* decision? Why wasn't it up to me? Why didn't I get to do the rejecting? But how would I have ended the evening? I was grateful to have been spared that decision. I should never have mentioned Ellsberg's kids and ex-wife. I knew nothing about it. I'd been trying to sound knowing. "Thanks," I said. "That was fun. You should probably get some sleep."

He said, "I really do apologize. The poker game did me in. Poker stirs up a lot of swampy residue. It brings me right back to the poker games with the CIA guys at Dr. Strangelove's villa in Saigon. It's the five-card-draw part of my post-Vietnam syndrome." He smiled.

That got my attention. I'd been distracted, trying to decide whether I was hurt or disappointed or indifferent to the fact that the evening was ending so lukewarmly. But if I wanted to be someone on whom nothing is wasted, I needed to listen. The story of what it was like to play poker with spies in Saigon wasn't exactly *nothing*.

Tony stared out the windshield more steadily than he had when he was driving. I thought of Henry and Grace asleep one flight up. Would they hear Tony's car idling? Would Grace wake up and look out the window and see us parked in front?

"The second time I went to Saigon, there was a weekly poker game in the private villa of Dr. Strangelove, RAND's top dog in Vietnam.

"My first boss had been a good guy, but they'd let him go. I heard that after he got the intel on the Vietnamese, he said, 'If what you're telling me is true, we're fighting on the wrong side.'

"Dr. Strangelove had taken his place. You've seen the movie, right?"

Everyone had seen Kubrick's film *Dr. Strangelove, or: How I Learned to Stop Worrying and Love the Bomb*, a comedy about the manic buildup to atomic Armageddon, a nuclear war between the Soviet Union and the United States.

"Of course." My arm shot up like Peter Sellers playing the title character, the German-born military strategist whose arm has a will of its own, twitching upward in a reflexive Hitler salute.

In an alternate scenario, Tony and I might have been kissing in the front seat, parked outside my apartment, deciding that maybe we *should* go back to Tony's place. Instead of which he was weeping quietly and I was imitating Peter Sellers imitating a Nazi.

Tony said, "Everyone thinks that character was based on Henry Kissinger, but my boss was Kissinger the Second, or maybe Kissinger was Dr. Strangelove the Second, another psycho refugee, except that my boss was handsome. Continental. Pipe smoker. Thick graying hair, swept back. Slouched. Ascot. Elbow-on-the-mantel kind of guy. Did I mention that he was a sadist? Being around him was like a nonstop hazing for some Prussian dueling club. At the poker games, no one was allowed to tell the new arrivals that they weren't supposed to win. If Dr. Strangelove lost to you, you'd be sent home. Bon voyage, sucker! Everybody watched the newcomers trying to figure out why we all played such shitty poker. Were their colleagues letting *them* win? Wrong answer! Bzzz. The door with the tiger behind it.

"I wasn't especially good at the game." He paused.

Did he want me to say, You *were* good?

I said, "You were fine. You played fine."

"The point was, I didn't particularly care, as you saw tonight, so losing wasn't a problem. I was never much of a gambler. Though with my statistics background, I could have counted cards and cleaned up. Only later did I wonder why we weren't asking each other why guys were being fired for beating the boss at poker.

"That's the kind of thing that kills me now. But it never seemed important enough. Or practical. Or . . . sensible. How would it help the Vietnamese if we lost our jobs? How would it help the United States if we got fired? Wasn't it better to be in the belly of the beast so at least we would know what the beast was doing? Maybe we could keep the beast from going wild. Wild-*er*. No matter what Dr. Strangelove did or said, not one of those guys, *us guys*, spoke up. Not once. We made small talk. We were polite. Yes, thank you, I'll have another mai tai, thanks. Another umbrella drink! Me, I wanted to stay in Vietnam. I wanted to do what I was doing. I laughed at the guy's jokes. Understand?"

I nodded, though I wasn't sure that I did. I'd never had a real job that I was afraid of losing. I'd taught Beginning Creative Writing because I didn't feel qualified to do anything else and was hardly able to do that, but mainly because no one else wanted to do it. I'd worked two high school summers as an assistant counselor at a day camp for blind kids on Long Island, and one college summer washing test tubes in a lab at the Bellevue morgue, where my father was a pathologist.

This was when suspicious deaths still came through the general autopsy room. My coworkers knew the details of every crime that had ever been committed in the city. I loved listening to them, and they liked telling their stories to anyone who hadn't heard them. I loved the Old Morgue, a gloomy brick McKim, Mead, and White building. I loved the culture of the autopsy room, the dark jokes about—and the respect for—the dead. Anyway, I was temporary. Everyone understood that my job would end when school began. My father had gotten me the job. There was no chance that I'd be fired.

I didn't tell Tony about any of that. I was in the front seat of an antiwar hero's car, imitating Nazis and thinking about the morgue. I was afraid of saying anything he might find creepy or depressing.

Tony got out and walked around the car, opened the door for me, and as I got out, he bowed slightly, a gentlemanly bow, half ironic, half real. By 1974, feminism had made us suspect male chivalry, with its subtext of power and condescension. But I knew that Tony was trying to be nice. I reminded myself that he came from a slightly older generation.

Instead of coming closer for a goodbye hug or kiss, he moved away, his hands in his pockets, his shoulders slightly arched. It was how Clyde Barrow stands in the photo, slouched back, half smiling at Bonnie Parker.

He said, "Are you free tomorrow night? I can pick you up here at eight."

It felt more like a reprieve than a date.

"Sure," I said. "That would be great."

"See you tomorrow," I said, but he had already sped off, checking his rearview mirror, though the dark street was empty.

A famous antiwar hero. Those words are like a time machine, rocketing passengers back to a time when activists were our lodestars. They were *doing something.* They inspired us with their willingness to sacrifice whatever was needed. Martin Luther King radiated courage, grace, and the grief of knowing that, as he said, he might not live to reach the Promised Land. Malcolm X was assassinated in the Audubon Ballroom. The Berrigan brothers were arrested and jailed for burning draft board files. Muhammad Ali resisted the draft and was banned from boxing for years. The Chicago Seven were tried for conspiracy to incite a riot. People changed their lives—and gave their lives—to end racism and stop the Vietnam War. They were living the way we thought we should live, the way we would have been living if we were a little braver, a little older, if circumstances were different, if we'd had more courageous lovers and more committed friends.

By the time I met Tony, he was still antiwar royalty, not as well-known as he had been, but still. For some of us, antiwar heroes were celebrities of a higher order than rock stars and actors, without the taint of having compromised, without the suspicion that their reputation had been created by an industry or a machine. They were famous for being brave, for doing the right thing. Stealing the Pentagon Papers had been a heroic act.

Henry had met Tony in Los Angeles in 1970, the year before the Pentagon Papers became national news. A mutual friend asked him to help carry boxes of photocopies out to the trunk of Tony's car, parked outside a flower shop that never seemed to do any business.

Henry loved to talk about how Tony had Tom Sawyered him

into committing a felony, especially after the charges against Tony and Ellsberg were dropped and Henry was no longer concerned about his own role, however minor, in a federal crime.

Tony Russo and Daniel Ellsberg were popular figures, whistleblowers who had provided massive evidence to support a position that, by that point, most Americans agreed on: We had no business killing the Vietnamese and sacrificing our soldiers just to keep a small country from becoming independent.

And yet the war continued. Nixon was bombing Cambodia. The war being fought on the other side of the world remained present for us, in our thoughts and imaginations. We watched it on the evening news, the way that, in 2022, we watched the war in Ukraine, except that it was *our* soldiers using chemical weapons, killing civilians, setting homes on fire. When the Vietnam War came into our living rooms, the soldier torching the thatched hut with his Zippo lighter became a media star.

My friends and I kept going to demonstrations, making posters. The protestors who sat down in the street and refused to move were arrested. In May 1971, a massive antiwar rally shut down Washington, DC. The local police and the National Guard were called in, and demonstrators were beaten and imprisoned.

Our heroes went to jail. Some moved to Canada rather than go to Vietnam. The movement ebbed and swelled with each downturn and escalation of the fighting, but our conviction never wavered. We wanted the war to end.

During the eleven years that the war in Vietnam lasted, we did what we could. Pretending to be one of the fox-trotting couples on the popular TV special *New Year's Eve Live from the Waldorf Astoria*, my friend and his girlfriend unfurled a banner that said "Stop Bombing Hanoi." Guy Lombardo, the bandleader, tried to hit them with his baton. They got six seconds of airtime. They were briefly detained by the hotel-security cops, one of whom said that he'd quit Columbia—where student protests were common—and had come to work for the hotel to get away from crap like that. That same friend would later scale the Pentagon walls at a demonstration.

Tony had done more to stop the war than anyone I knew. He'd wrecked his career. He had been followed, wiretapped, harassed, jailed, and assaulted. He had gone from being a respected and highly paid engineer, economist, and data analyst to being unemployed and, he feared, unemployable.

By the time I met Tony at Henry and Grace's, Nixon had been reelected in a landslide victory, which Tony interpreted as a sign that he might have ruined his career for nothing, that nothing he'd done had worked. But, as he often said, he had learned from the North Vietnamese that every defeat was a signpost on the road to victory and freedom.

The story that went around was that Ellsberg asked Tony if he knew where they could find a photocopy machine.

And Tony said, "I have just the place."

There was a Xerox machine at the office of his girlfriend, Lynda Sinay, who had her own business, an advertising agency above a flower shop. She ran the office herself, so it seemed private and safe. One night early on, Sinay's burglar alarm went off. Two policemen showed up, checked Tony's ID, gave the place a superficial once-over, and left.

There's a film of Tony talking about his near escape on that first night: "I'd just started copying. I was working away, and there was a knock on the door. I looked out, and there were two guys from the LAPD standing there. I said to myself, These guys are really good."

The nervy young woman who let her whistleblower boyfriend and his buddy photocopy seven thousand pages of top secret documents in her office has become part of the story's mystique. It's possible that Lynda Sinay was in love with Tony—she said that she'd thought he would "save her" from her political naivete—or a little in love with both Tony and Dan and their outlaw mission. Later she explained that she wanted to end the war, and she believed that Dan and Tony were working to make that happen. Though the papers were marked "Top Secret," she was shocked when she was summoned before the grand jury as an unindicted co-conspirator.

Prosecutors spent two years attempting to try and convict her, but eventually the charges were dropped. Lynda Sinay married a man named Resnick, and together they started a succession of lucrative businesses that now include Fiji Water, Pom (the pomegranate drink), and Halos, the mandarin oranges that are on my kitchen table now. She and her husband are major philanthropists who have donated millions to scientific and cultural institutions.

Tony liked to say that he'd been the devil in Dan's ear, telling him to leak the papers to the press because the American people needed to know how their government had lied to them. They both believed that exposing the government's lies would help end the war. They were certain that Americans would be so *horrified* to hear that a president *lied* that the entire population would rise up and demand an end to the fighting in Asia.

I hesitate to say *my generation* or to generalize about *any* generation, Boomers or Millennials, Generation X or Y or Z, because such a wide range of humans are born around the same time and lead such different lives. I try not to use the word *generation*, but to rely on the first-person plural, *we*, meaning a subset of people who were more or less young then and had similar ideas. Radicals, hippies, feminists, artists, activists, students, ordinary people who believed that the war was wrong.

I never liked the word *counterculture* either. It's like *Oriental* in that it defines something in relation to something else. *Oriental*—east of what? *Counterculture*—counter to what? What if we *were* the culture and not its opponent?

And who were *we*, that first-person plural? Kids whose mothers got pregnant soon after our fathers came home from the war. Kids whose parents had lived through the Depression and World War II and who saw a brighter future ahead for their brand-new families in their brand-new houses with their brand-new dishwashers and washing machines. Their amazing new televisions! Kids whose parents believed that we had achieved a lasting peace, freedom and prosperity for all, who believed that there would be enough jobs, enough food on the table, family vacations. Kids whose parents dreamed of sending them to college, where they would acquire the knowledge and skills required to climb the newly extended ladder. Kids whose parents believed that our government cared about us, that our leaders had desegregated public schools and were improving our educational system so that we could keep pace with—keep ahead of—the Russians.

Kids who watched the McCarthy hearings on our new TVs.

Black kids growing up in the Jim Crow South. Kids who watched Bull Connor, Birmingham's commissioner of public safety, sic his snarling attack dogs on Black civil rights demonstrators. Kids whose school days were interrupted by announcements on the loudspeakers ordering us to crouch under our desks for drills that would protect us from the atomic bomb. Kids who knew that our desks were not going to protect us from the A-bomb, which meant that our parents and teachers were lying.

Kids who loved Elvis Presley, who listened to Black music, who mourned James Dean. Kids who experimented with the drugs that our parents said would make us go insane and spend the rest of our lives in mental hospitals.

Kids who were deciding that our elders lied about everything, or almost. Kids who knew that our government didn't care about us, that class and racial divides were solid and more or less impermeable; kids who knew that there was never going to be peace as long as someone could make money from war; kids who knew that there was never going to be racial and economic equality because, no matter what they pretended, the selfish bigoted grown-ups didn't want it. If things were going to get better, it would be up to us.

Idealistic and hopeful and full of ourselves, admirable and naive, we thought that we could change society if we could only make our voices heard. We weren't just dreamy adolescents. We had proof that it could work. In 1968, there were student uprisings all over the world. There were youth riots in Mexico, Belgium, Italy, and Yugoslavia. Led by students and young activists, the Prague Spring marked the Czech people's attempt to leave the Eastern Bloc.

We weren't about to follow the rules, to keep quiet and do what we were told when we thought that we were being told to do something wrong. We spoke up. We did what we could.

The shah of Iran was my college graduation speaker, and—because we knew about his brutal secret police and his CIA connections—we wore black armbands and boycotted the ceremony. That May, students occupied Columbia University's administration building, demanding that the university quit buying up Harlem, dispossessing Black residents, and that the school cut its financial ties with the Defense Department. The Black Panther Party deployed their stylish, powerful charisma in public spaces and started a free breakfast program that scared the FBI into calling them "America's Number One Terrorist Group."

We knew that the struggle was not the same for white people and people of color, but we believed that we had common ground. Vietnam was a problem for us all. White and Black leaders spoke out against it. The Black Panthers donated to Tony Russo's defense fund. Jean Genet traveled with the Panthers, working to recruit young white people to support the Panthers' defense. Bobby Seale was indicted for conspiracy as part of the Chicago Eight until his case was separated out. The committee to free the Soledad Brothers, three incarcerated Black men accused of killing a white prison guard in 1970, included Benjamin Spock and Angela Davis, Julian Bond and Allen Ginsberg. White and Black kids from all over the Bay Area crowded into the courtroom to watch the trial. Carloads of young people drove up to Marin County to pack the seats at the Angela Davis murder trial in the San Rafael courthouse. On YouTube, archival footage of the Davis arraignment includes scenes of Black Panthers and scraggly white kids lined up to pass through the metal detectors.

Demonstrating in support of the accused and attending their trials felt like a civic duty. Maybe our belief in a rapprochement across color and class lines was always wishful thinking, but at the time it seemed useful to proceed as if we shared at least some ideas and hopes for a more equitable future.

It was a time of earthquakes and aftershocks. Every few days brought a tremor that rattled and destabilized us before we'd recovered from the last. In the winter of 1968, the Tet Offensive made it clear that we were never going to win in Vietnam. That spring, Martin Luther King and Robert F. Kennedy were shot and killed. That summer, ten thousand people demonstrated against the war during the Democratic National Convention in Chicago. Films of cops beating protestors appeared nightly on the news.

Stanley Kubrick's *2001: A Space Odyssey* showed us a sterile future that we didn't want. Tom Wolfe's *The Electric Kool-Aid Acid Test* persuaded its readers that hippies traveling around in a school bus were taking more drugs and having more sex and way more fun than they were. The Beatles were only the most famous of the pilgrims who traveled East in search of enlightenment, smoked Afghan hash, painted Sanskrit letters on their foreheads, and swapped horror stories about Turkish border guards. Timothy Leary was advising us to turn on, tune in, drop out. The consequences of dropping out would be sorted out later. After the revolution, we could stay high and harvest soybeans for a month every summer.

We believed that there was a better idea out there in the ether, and that if we only worked hard enough and thought deeply enough, we would find solutions so that we could all be equal, so that no one had to be poor or hungry, so that we didn't have to go to war in countries that didn't want or need us. We believed that compassion would prevail. Racism and colonialism would wither away and die. Gandhi and Martin Luther King had proven that nonviolence could succeed. The world had thanked them by killing them, but others would take their place.

We were very young and very fired up. We didn't know what the answers were, but we believed we could find them. We believed that everyone should be heard and respected, that everyone had something to say. You didn't have to own a bicycle; you could share, like they did (we'd heard) in Amsterdam. We believed health care should be free; maybe we could have something like China's "barefoot doctors" traveling from province to province, treating everyone in need. Volunteer clinics operated in storefronts. No appointment necessary. We believed in democracy, a true democracy, not the oligarchy that we lived in.

We believed that love was the strongest emotion. We believed in the collective imagination. We knew what Hitler and Stalin had imagined, not long before we were born. But Hitler and Stalin were old and dead, and we were young and alive. We were better.

"The big idea we had—though heaven knows it wasn't new—was freedom," writes Jenny Diski, in her dazzling book, *The Sixties*, "liberty, permission, a great enlarging of human possibilities beyond the old politenesses and restrictions. But it was an idea we failed to think through. It was a failure of thought essentially, rather than a failure of imagination. We were completely wrong-footed when the Sixties turned inexorably into the Eighties. With Margaret Thatcher and Ronald Reagan presiding, our favourite words—freedom, liberty, permission—were bandied about anew and dressed in clothes that made them unrecognizable to us."

The Vietnam War became the symbol and the reality of what had to change. We believed that we could make it happen; at least we had to try. You could stop a war, you could eradicate poverty, you could make America face up to its racism. Every kid could grow up to be Gandhi, Angela Davis, or Che Guevara. The Black Panthers and the Young Lords knew who ran the country and who didn't, and what America needed to do in order to become a more just and equitable society.

If the late '60s were about believing in the possibility of funda-
mental change, the 1970s were about the dawning realization
that the changes we'd wanted weren't going to happen. Columbia University was not going to stop buying up Harlem. As the
Vietnam War spread to Laos and Cambodia, the lies about it
became more deadly. Separated from his co-defendants in the
Chicago Eight trial, the Black Panther leader Bobby Seale was
bound and gagged in the courtroom.

Russian tanks ended the Prague Spring. The Black Panther
leaders were arrested or killed. The photo of the girl kneeling
on the ground at Kent State University, keening over a dead
demonstrator, was everywhere. For a while.

The democratically elected Salvador Allende was over-
thrown in Chile before he could nationalize the mines and
industries, threatening multinational profits. The murderous
dictator Augusto Pinochet, supported by Henry Kissinger, was
installed in Allende's place. By the early 1970s, almost half of
Black Americans were living below the poverty line.

Charlie Manson's cult-commune killing spree, the explosion
that killed three Weathermen and blew up a Greenwich Village
townhouse, the murder at the Rolling Stones' Altamont Speed-
way concert—these heavily reported events were good news to
conservatives who saw them as proof that they'd been right all
along. Hippie ninja assassins were waiting to murder us in our
beds and write "Death to Pigs" in our blood, on the bedroom
wall. The Zebra killers—a small gang of Black men targeting
random San Franciscans—quickened the pulse of white fear,
even as the Symbionese Liberation Army accused the establishment of inventing the Zebra killers as an excuse to launch a race

war. The murders and deaths, the racist violence, the thickening atmosphere of chaos and violence and dread were catnip to the industrialists and right-wing ideologues who had already begun strategizing their long game for the economy and the planet.

We'd heard about the domino theory: A single defeat in one country would mean that every country would fall, like a line of dominoes, to the communist invaders. But when the dominoes toppled, the winner of the game wasn't global communism, but Ronald Reagan, George Bush, and Margaret Thatcher, the petrochemical industry, corporations, and Big Pharma.

Money won't change you, James Brown sang, but he must have noticed that it could. We wanted to think that money would eventually matter less, or not at all, even when Marx told us that, as far as history was concerned, it was the only thing that did. We believed that education and childcare should be freely available. That no one should be hungry or poor. We were dreaming a whole new future, as glorious and improbable as Oz.

Some of us were more pragmatic. An entrepreneurial friend made money selling blankets at the 1969 Woodstock music festival. Perhaps the dream of peace and freedom, of equality and transparency, was always a delusion, mass hysteria, like tulip mania or the Children's Crusade. The odds were against our high-minded plans. The odds were on uncontrolled capitalism. The seeds of government surveillance—wiretaps, spying, undercover provocateurs, violations of due process—had been planted and blossomed when Robert F. Kennedy (a hero of Daniel Ellsberg's) was attorney general.

Nothing much would change except that we would get older and more complacent, lulled by our jobs, our kids, seduced by our creature comforts into thinking that the status quo was pretty much okay, not ideal, but it worked, especially if you were white and middle class. The media was no longer biting the hand that fed it, but learning to kiss it. News providers began to avoid the "unbalanced" stories that showed its advertisers and board members in an unflattering light.

Marx understood that money drove history, but chose not to believe that wanting more and more was part of human nature, along with the reluctance to share. Soviet leaders wore ermine coats while the proletariat froze. We believed in equality, in ending poverty and injustice, but when we got old enough to buy houses, few of us, as far as I know, invited the homeless to live there.

That everything could be commodified came as a slow-motion surprise, a shock that happened so gradually we hardly even noticed, not even when you could buy Che Guevara T-shirts at the county fair and the car wash. The ideals of the '60s were sorted and reconfigured for profit. The attainable goals were excised along with those that were difficult, impractical, impossible to achieve. The surge of power we got from our victories—the end of the Vietnam War, the 1973 ruling of *Roe v. Wade*—were replaced by the more reliable dopamine hits of spending and acquisition.

By 1974, the ground beneath us had shifted and split along fault lines that opened up everywhere. It was as if the culture was saying, You commie hippies with your crazy ideas about peace and love and freedom, your brains were fried by drugs and excessive sex, and you're bad for business. So we're not going to take it. All we have to do is make some threats, authorize a few wiretaps, kill a few Black leaders. There's money to be made, fame and power to grab, and you're not going to get it.

It took me years—decades—to understand what had happened.

When my college class returned to Harvard for its twenty-fifth reunion in 1993, Colin Powell, the chairman of the Joint Chiefs of Staff, was the commencement speaker. This was right after he approved the "don't ask, don't tell" policy, restricting the freedoms of gay people in the military. At the ceremony, my class—the same people who protested the shah of Iran and boycotted our undergrad graduation, the formerly scruffy kids who had shouted down Defense Secretary Robert McNamara when he came to speak in Cambridge—was thanked by Harvard's president for their extremely generous alumni contributions.

That contribution—that disposable wealth—was what had happened. The college had graduated its legacy aristocrats and boosted a phalanx of public school kids into the upper middle class. Colin Powell got a standing ovation, as did the most popular degree recipient, Julia Child.

I took my two sons to the reunion. They asked why I didn't know anyone there. I said that my friends hadn't bothered to come. I didn't mention that several were dead; others had left the country. One was in Africa; another would soon die in Thailand.

Even so, I enjoyed the reunion. At first my classmates scared me. Many had become people whom I could imagine rejecting my application for a bank loan. But in fact they were friendly and interesting, and they didn't seem to mind our lack of shared college memories.

Maybe it helped that they knew I was writing about the reunion for *Vogue*. The editors sent a photographer with an eye for the grotesque, which suggested that someone imagined the class of 1968 in headbands and beads, paunchy bald investment bankers boogying to Jefferson Airplane under a spinning disco ball. In fact there were plenty of lawyers, hedge fund managers, and academic scientists, but no headbands and beads, no disco ball.

It turned out that *Vogue* hadn't sent me to write a political essay about the gap between our boycott of the shah and our standing ovation for Colin Powell. They wanted to know what people *wore*, if we'd needed to let out the seams of our bell-bottom jeans, paisley shirts, and fringed denim jackets. The magazine killed the piece. I can't remember why. I suspect that the photos weren't geeky enough.

I'd known Henry and Grace for a long time, and I liked them a lot. Henry was a high school friend of my soon-to-be ex-husband's, and he'd lived with us for a few months, in Massachusetts, where he had come to get out of the draft. Then he'd moved back to San Francisco.

The first time I crossed the country and rented Henry and Grace's sunny guest bedroom through the fall and the mild (compared to Boston) Northern California winter was in the summer of 1972. I'd been in flight from Cambridge, where I'd become unable to leave my apartment without consulting the I Ching, the Confucian Book of Changes.

It says something about me and my friends, about the era in which we lived, that so many of us owned a copy of the I Ching. With its dove gray Art Deco–design dust jacket, it looks like an edition that the Woolfs and Hogarth Press might have published. Written centuries before Christ, the book contains a system of divination based on a stack of six parallel lines, straight or broken, each corresponding to an image (the Lake, Fire on the Mountain) and a paragraph of poetic philosophy and vague advice. You ask the oracle a question, and it answers via a hexagram derived by passing yarrow stalks from hand to hand or flipping three coins.

In those days, I believed, or wanted to believe, that the future could be foretold. Maybe it's only human to want to see what lies ahead. The freedom to dabble in the occult went along with the other freedoms we claimed for ourselves: the freedom to believe, simultaneously and without irony, in astrology, in evolution, in the power of great art, and in Engels's ideas about the origin of the family. Necromancy seemed like a semi-logical declaration of independence: If we didn't believe the answers we got from our parents and teachers, we'd look for new explanations in mysticism, politics, Eastern philosophy, and drugs.

We suspected our elders of blindness and greed. We took nothing they told us on faith. We agreed not to trust anyone over thirty, but we made exceptions for Picasso, Chuck Berry, and Jeanne Moreau. We were determined to figure things out for ourselves. We were our own science experiments, researching the paranormal. Who could say that ancient thought systems might not hold the key to the future? Millions of people still had faith in these methods of fortune-telling and divination. Could they all be wrong?

I read tarot cards. I cast the I Ching. I had a friend who could guess someone's astrological sign after talking to them for five minutes.

People consulted the I Ching for many reasons, often for permission to do what they planned to do anyway: Should I sleep with my husband's best friend? Undertaking brings good fortune. Remorse disappears. Most of us had only a vague idea of the oracle's history and significance, but I think it did us good, or some good, to read the eloquent Confucian text and its fallback message: Perseverance furthers.

Some people took its advice more seriously than others. A friend called to say she'd been terrified by an ominous hexagram. We agreed: It's only a book! I was ashamed to tell her that I couldn't leave my apartment in Cambridge without its reassurance. Often I had to root around in the couch cushions to find the pennies I needed to cast a hexagram.

Maybe it was a kind of OCD, like having to touch the doorknob a certain number of times before I could open the door. But this was before we knew the acronyms that now so readily come to mind when we evaluate our own mental health and diagnose our loved ones.

Now someone as compulsive and unhappy as I was then would probably be medicated. But I was too proud or stubborn or shy to look for a name for my problem. And psychopharmacology was nowhere near what it is today. We knew people who took Valium, mother's little helper—who wanted to take *that*? Weed and psychedelics were fine, speed and coke in moderation, but pills had been invented to turn housewives into zombies. Junkies had a kind of social cachet, an aura of doomed romance, but we worried when our friends drifted into hard drugs; by then, a few people I knew had overdosed and died.

I suppose there was a kind of instability, what we would now call bipolarity, in the way that, during those years, I veered between periods of paralyzing dread and times of being dangerously trusting and even indifferent to danger. For months, I'd see myself as a rebel and an outlaw, and then, in the months that followed, as someone hiding in a corner or looking for a corner to hide in.

I was afraid that the needle would keep swinging between those extremes, or that it would stop on one side or the other. What I was working toward, what I hoped, was for my psyche to stay intact, bouncing comfortably in the middle between recklessness and terror, between safety and disaster.

In Cambridge I'd had an imaginary psychiatrist, a hostile university health-services doctor, a middle-aged man with the dark-rimmed glasses, white lab coat, and graying hair of a family doc on TV. When I try to remember how I pictured him, I see Henry Kissinger's face.

During the conversations—the sessions—I had with him in my mind, the imaginary doctor told me that I'd given myself agoraphobia by repressing my desire to walk away from graduate school, my husband, my apartment, my life. I imagined agreeing but arguing (weakly) in my defense that I hadn't planned on moving around the corner from a section of Kirkland Street that had apparently been designated as a safe space for flashers to park their cars and expose themselves to the women who walked by. I can still see the men's expressions when I saw what they meant me to see, the cruel goofy smiles or hard stares that said: Now we have a secret.

Farther up Kirkland Street was the supermarket where Julia Child was best friends with the butcher. Sometimes I passed the famous couple on the street: the gangly, chatty celebrity cook and her attentive husband. But the market was one of the places to which, as the circle of dread contracted, I was afraid to go. First the English department, then my classes, then anywhere beyond my apartment, anywhere but my bed.

The summer I left Cambridge, my husband spent a month in California. The plan was that he would come back, and we would switch. I would go out West and return before school started again.

That summer, when he was gone, there were violent thunderstorms every afternoon. Four, four thirty. Every single day. There was nothing to do but wait them out. What if the neighbor's dead willow tree was struck by lightning and fell on our house? Sometimes the electricity failed, and I'd pull the blankets over my head.

One of the few places to which I could still go was the apartment of a friend's boyfriend, whom I slept with because he told me that Bob Dylan's "I'll Keep It with Mine" was a song about God.

He played records for me. His favorite songs, or so he said, were Laura Nyro and LaBelle harmonizing on "I Met Him on a Sunday" and Billie Holiday singing "Don't Explain," two songs that spanned the range of how a woman in love could behave. In the first, she tells her boyfriend to get lost after he stands her up, just once. In the second, a woman tells her lover, Go ahead. Hurt me. I'll never leave. You don't even have to offer a plausible explanation. How romantic. How attractive.

I felt guilty for betraying my friend, but the high drama was a welcome distraction. For a while, I thought that I was in love, and when I listened to Janis Joplin and Joni Mitchell, they seemed to be saying that when love called, you had to answer, no matter where it took you, no matter what it made you do.

I had intense, short-lived crushes on unavailable men. The biology-department lab assistant who had taken so many psychoactive drugs on a research trip to the Amazon that he could barely speak. The Argentinean hippie goldsmith who made our wedding rings. The Vietnam vet who'd been on a bomb-demolition squad and jumped whenever someone popped a champagne cork.

One night a gay friend (whom I also had a crush on) came over for dinner. He arrived early. I was listening to Joni Mitchell. Together we listened to "The Last Time I Saw Richard."

My friend, a bright, optimistic spirit, said, "Is *this* what you've been listening to? No wonder you're so unhappy."

My imaginary health-services psychiatrist said, "You're living a life meant for someone else."

He (that is, I) was right. This wasn't my real life. I was not really a graduate student. I was not really a graduate student's wife. I wasn't married to my husband. I wasn't actually falling in love with every damaged eccentric I met. I was not actually cheating on my friend with her boyfriend.

I was just pretending to *be* all those things, to *do* all those things. But knowing all that was useless unless someone could show me the real life, the true life, the life I was meant to live—the life that I was looking for when I went to San Francisco.

Statistics tell us that most people lie to their doctors. I lied to my imaginary psychiatrist. I chose not to mention that "this" had happened to me once before. What was "this"? The agoraphobia, the dull terror, the fear that I could spend the rest of my life holed up in a Cambridge apartment, like the mad female recluses in my favorite books: Miss Havisham without the wedding cake. Emily Dickinson without the wild genius. Mr. Rochester's wife without, I hoped, burning up in the attic.

The first—let's call it an episode—began during my first year in graduate school, in the fall of 1968. I was studying medieval English literature, not the most practical subject. But I loved the oddness and beauty of the narratives, the pared-down, off-center ways in which they told stories, the mysterious characters whose behavior contradicted the most basic tenets of modern psychology. I loved the bloody Icelandic sagas with their spooky prophecies, irresistible witches, long-simmering feuds and revenges.

I'd stayed in Cambridge for grad school partly because Harvard offered me a fellowship but mostly because I'd married my college boyfriend, and he had already begun graduate study at Harvard. Also I didn't know what else to do or where else to go.

I no longer loved my husband, if I ever had. I liked his eccentric talented friends, his passion for R. Crumb and underground comics, for Black music, for obscure groups and singers: Sugar Pie DeSanto, Shorty Long, Barbara Lewis. In high school my friends and I spent hours listening to early Motown and '50s doo-wop, and when I discovered that none of the women in my dorm knew who James Brown was, I knew that I had wound up in the wrong place, a conviction that would come and go as long as I lived in Cambridge. I liked that my husband came from the West and introduced me to my first artichoke.

At first my husband (then my boyfriend) and I used to make each other laugh, but that had pretty much stopped. We used to get high and have sex, but now we mostly argued, even when we were high or after sex. They were the kind of arguments you have when you are totally bored with a person and can admit anything except that. I'd known that the marriage was a terrible idea, but it had seemed like too much trouble—too embarrassing—to call off the wedding.

The night before the ceremony, my mother said, "You don't have to go through with this," and I said, "Whatever. You've sent out the invitations and bought all the food."

I'd taken the path of least resistance. I got married because I'd said I would. I'd stayed in school because I'd realized that I could read Victorian novels and Icelandic sagas, hang out with my friends, get high, watch TV—and do well in school without having to work very hard. I stayed married because it seemed so difficult to make the decision to leave and split everything up and find a new place to live. My husband wasn't really that bad. He wasn't violent or cruel. We just weren't happy together.

It was a privileged life, I knew. I was a writer. I'd published a book. I'd gotten some recognition. So why should it have felt as if I was struggling not to drown? Why? Because I was in my twenties. A friend says, It's a time of suffering. People in their twenties spend so much of their time just trying to figure out where the floor is.

In those days, my favorite poem was one of John Berryman's *77 Dream Songs.*

It begins:

Life, friends, is boring. We must not say so.
After all, the sky flashes, the great sea yearns,
we ourselves flash and yearn,
and moreover my mother told me as a boy
(repeatingly) 'Ever to confess you're bored
means you have no

Inner Resources.' I conclude now I have no
inner resources, because I am heavy bored.

I used to read it to my husband. And I would laugh, in case he didn't get the point. He got the point. I wanted him to be as miserable as I was. To let him know how bored I was, in case he hadn't noticed. He'd noticed. That was how I tormented my husband: by weaponizing John Berryman.

Our first married-couple apartment looked out on Cambridge Common, a park through which I had been chased twice, by strangers with their flies unzipped. If I'm making Cambridge sound like a magnet for sex offenders, that's what it was then, and may still be. Neighborhoods with large populations of female students often have that effect.

The lobby of our building was furnished and lit like a funeral home presided over by the elderly Irish janitor who knew everything that happened in the building, and didn't like me. He openly hated Blacks and Jews, and he'd figured out I was Jewish. He had a radar for it. Once, he asked me why "you Jewish people" ate so much Chinese takeout. Do your people really believe that eating cat is better than eating pork? He knew that someone at our house watched a lot of TV and smoked a lot of dope, which was strictly illegal. You could go to jail, even if you were white. I had a recurring dream in which old Mr. Foley turned me in to the cops.

The summer after graduation, the summer of the Chicago riots, my college friends—fans of Tina Turner, Sly Stone, Aubrey Beardsley, Sylvia Plath, S. Clay Wilson, Hitchcock, and psychedelic drugs—went off to Manhattan and Europe. In September they were replaced by graduate student pod-people having lunch at the same tables where my friends used to eat. In the entering class were several nuns and seminarians, along with some academic mean girls, and young men who exuded the friendly chill of Mormon missionaries. They didn't read what I read; they didn't like what I liked. We couldn't talk about books, films, music, or TV.

In just a few months I'd changed from being a moderately friendly person into a pathologically shy one. I couldn't follow the thread of ordinary conversation. I never knew what to say. How was I supposed to answer if someone asked me how I was? When one of my college friends returned from Oxford that winter, it was too late to salvage the wreck I'd become.

I asked my husband, "If you just met me, what would you think I was like?"

He said, "What a stupid question. Why are you even asking?"

I'd felt that I'd been demoted from a promising undergraduate to one of the delusional drones who actually imagined that someday we were going to take our professors' places. Our teachers knew what their graduate students were hoping and plotting, and they tormented us, revealing mean streaks they'd hidden from their college students. The distinguished Chaucer scholar forced a blushing nun to translate, aloud, the scene in "The Miller's Tale" in which the adulterous lover sticks his ass out the window and farts on his rival. The tough-talking department chairman told me how disappointed he was when "one of ours" (he meant someone who'd gone to Harvard as an undergraduate) "fucked up" (he meant missing classes, not handing in papers) as badly as I did. It would have been different, he said, if I'd gone to . . . well . . . Villanova.

Another attempt at conversation that went nowhere involved my efforts to persuade my graduate classmates to read *One Hundred Years of Solitude*, recently published in Gregory Rabassa's stellar translation. I'd memorized the first sentence: "Many years later, as he faced the firing squad, Colonel Aureliano Buendía was to remember that distant afternoon when his father took him to discover ice." I repeated it over and over in my head, like a mantra that soothed me as I sat mutely in class. I couldn't convince anyone to read it. Maybe my classmates suspected my motives, and they would have been right. I saw the novel as a damning critique of them and everything they stood for: García Márquez's delight in storytelling was so much juicier and more alive than the pretentious seminars designed (I thought) to make literature seem competitive, arid, and joyless.

García Márquez's novel was making me want to become a writer. Populating a world with characters and coming up with plot turns seemed like pure pleasure. I'd taken a few writing classes in college. James Alan McPherson, then attending Harvard Law School, was a student in one of those seminars, and after we heard his brilliant story "Gold Coast," about a janitor almost exactly like the one in my building, I wrote nothing for the rest of the semester. It wasn't much of a loss. I'd been writing wistful fiction about the romantic breakups that I should have been having in real life.

That first year in graduate school, I wrote a little fiction, lying in bed, with the TV on: stories in which I couldn't get my characters to leave the house. My young female narrators had tough shells but were secretly wan and morose.

By November I'd stopped getting out of bed except for a twice weekly Intermediate Latin class (we were reading Ovid's *Metamorphoses*, which I loved) and a weekly seminar on *Sir Gawain and the Green Knight*, taught by the playwright William Alfred, who had a beautiful reading voice and who seemed like a model human being.

Also I attended the required Beginning German class that met daily at eight in the morning, because I needed a reason, any reason, to get out of bed, and because I hoped that memorizing German grammar would keep my brain from melting into meat glue. That part of the day suggested that my survival instinct was still intact, sending out faint signals. But by afternoon the signals sputtered out, the spirit failed me, and I'd go home and get into bed and get high and stare at the TV for the rest of the day and fall asleep watching Dick Cavett.

If I'd mentioned any of that, the imaginary doctor might have asked if I saw any connection between the two episodes of agoraphobia. Could my problems possibly be related to . . . graduate school? And . . . marriage? Admitting that would have meant changing my life, and I wasn't ready. It was okay, it was fine, I could live the way I was living until I no longer could. I resigned myself to leading someone else's life—marriage, academia—until another option or solution appeared.

One summer afternoon, the I Ching said, Duration. It furthers one to have somewhere to go.

I made myself walk to Harvard Square. I told myself that all I had to do was to get that far, and then I could turn around and come home and get back into bed.

Crossing Boylston Street, I saw crowds gathered around transistor radios and a TV that had been set up in a store window. People were crying.

American astronauts had just landed on the moon.

I began to cry too. It felt cozy and surprisingly comforting, weeping in public—not, in my case, because I was so moved by our giant step for mankind, but because my life should have begun and hadn't, because I had absolutely no idea where I belonged in the universe or what I was going to do.

That first year I lived with Henry and Grace in San Francisco, I'd caught a ride with three friends driving across the country from Cambridge to California. In those days someone was always driving from coast to coast. Gas was cheaper. People felt fine driving long distances in a car with no air-conditioning and windows that didn't open and rusted-out holes in the floor through which you could watch the wheels turn underneath.

It was late August when we left. The summer was ending. I don't know why I agreed to go with my friends, or why traveling to San Francisco seemed so much safer than walking around the block in Cambridge. Most of the time I would be in a car with people I trusted. Roadside bathrooms scared me, but I would tough it out. All four of us would sleep—economically, chastely—in one motel room with two beds. We would drive across the badlands and through the red rock country in Arizona.

My survival instinct was telling me: You need to be somewhere far away. You need to leave here *now*.

I told my husband that I would be coming back East when school resumed in September, and then we would find another apartment. Our arguments—the petty cruelties, the intentionally mean and fake-innocent betrayals, the real and imaginary love affairs with other people—all of that would stop.

In all fairness, even if we'd been more compatible or more in love, our timing couldn't have been worse. Monogamy is always a serious commitment, more challenging for some than for others. But promising lifelong fidelity when you are young and in the midst of a so-called sexual revolution was way beyond our powers. The music we loved had come to seem like a reproach, a reminder: Someone is in love, but it isn't you, and you will never feel like that again. Monogamy seemed embarrassing, hopelessly square and old-fashioned. The culture encouraged, expected, and all but insisted on erotic restlessness. Sex was free; sex was everywhere, a source of wonder, pleasure, and heat without the chilling effect of familiarity and repetition.

Only later, after the way that things ended with Tony, did I begin to think there was anything irresponsible or unkind about my not having told my husband that I was leaving for good.

We agreed that we just needed a few weeks apart, and a continent between us. But when my husband wasn't paying attention, which was all the time, I packed up everything I owned and stored most of it with my parents in New York. I thought about leaving the I Ching in Cambridge along with the cigarettes I was determined to quit, but I took the book and a carton of Gauloises, in case I couldn't get them in California.

I'd gotten married for the same reasons that, over time, have guided many of my wrong decisions. Because agreeing is easier than refusing, because saying yes makes everyone happier than saying no. Maybe I also wanted the world to know that a man, any man, wanted to marry me. Now, when I see photos of myself at that age, I think I must have been insane to look in the mirror and see the ugly duckling I thought I saw.

Also there was this: Despite our belief in women's liberation, in breaking free from the prison of conventional gender roles, marriage and family remained markers of female success, even among women—rebels and feminists—who no longer believed that was true. Our clothes were looser, our hair longer, we wore Frye boots instead of high heels, but in many ways it could have been the 1950s. Glamorous, aristocratic, photogenic Jackie and John F. Kennedy, reigning in the White House, had been the bride and groom atop the wedding cake until his assassination smashed it.

I was excited and grateful when feminism shone a light on what had always existed, hidden in plain sight. Other women had noticed the meat market creepiness of the Miss America pageant, the sex-doll Playboy bunnies programmed to combine the servile, the slutty, and the unobtainable. We'd registered the condescension of the men who meant it when they called women *girls*, who believed—and treated us as if—we were congenitally stupid. The proof of our stupidity was that we didn't have a penis! Other women had noticed that, even if we worked outside the home, we were still responsible for the housework, the cooking, and the childcare. Other women had observed that we were being paid less than our male coworkers and that women of color were earning least of all. It was real; those were facts. It was a relief to find out that we were not alone, that others shared our concerns, that we weren't just *hypersensitive*, as women are so often accused of being.

Early in 1972, several months before I left my husband and first left Cambridge for California, I joined a women's consciousness-raising group.

At our initial meeting it emerged that none of us, not one, had ever seen a male relative use a vacuum cleaner. It surprised me that I couldn't recall my father once having helped with the housework. Both he and my mother were doctors. Both worked full-time at hospitals and clinics. I was less surprised by my father's inability to load the dishwasher than by the fact that I'd never noticed.

I loved my father, and it felt like a betrayal to mock him for not washing a coffee cup. No one had ever asked him to carry a dish as far as the sink. He had a brother and two sisters. My grandmother and my aunts had done all that. It was how things *were*.

I began to realize that *patriarchy*—that Old Testament word—was a reasonably accurate description of our household. My aunt, my mother's sister, a high school biology teacher, never married and lived with us, on the third floor of our house in Brooklyn. My father enjoyed the attention of a sort of harem: a loving wife, an adoring daughter, and a dependent (and also adoring) sister-in-law. I don't think it was ever clear to my father how my younger brother fit in. I was fine with *subverting* the patriarchy, with *undermining* the patriarchy. But *destroying* the patriarchy? Who would live in our house? It was an unusual sort of patriarchy, the power balance scrambled somewhat by the fact that the men and two women involved not only worked full-time but each had a demanding career. Even so, it was clear that my father was in charge. After dinner he went upstairs to read his medical journals.

My parents would have given anything for me, their only daughter, to become a doctor. I appreciated their faith in me, but it wasn't going to happen. Maybe if I hadn't been so bored and confused by biology, despite my kindly aunt's tutoring; maybe if I hadn't failed geology and done almost as badly in math; maybe if my high school chemistry teacher hadn't been so witchy and mean. Maybe if I hadn't had to fake the results from my high school science project, which involved dosing goldfish with liquid barbiturates I'd gotten from my mother. The Space Race with the Russians was ramping up science programs, transforming public education all over the country—but nothing had changed for decades in our small Quaker school.

Even if my parents were misguided in their desire for me to replicate their lives, I'm grateful for their raising me to believe that a girl could grow up to do anything she wanted—as long as it was what they wanted.

All the time I was married, I tried, I really tried. I tried to be the kind of woman, the kind of wife, I thought I was supposed to be. I cooked recipes from Julia Child, as my mother had done to prove that she could be a doctor and also a good wife, something that my father's parents had vocally and insultingly doubted. I made crêpes from scratch, stuffed with spinach, mushrooms, and heavy cream. My husband appreciated the effort; maybe he even liked them. I thought they tasted like soggy cardboard tubes filled with salty green library paste. He washed the dishes, but I did all the cooking. Later, when I stopped cooking, it was my job to order the Chinese takeout.

My parents wanted me to be a successful doctor married to a more successful doctor. But by the early 1970s, they'd resigned themselves: Their dreams were unlikely to come true. They were thrilled when my first book was published. They read it seriously, enjoyed it. They said smart and thoughtful things. They were thrilled by the reviews. But they knew the size of my book advance. Especially after I left my husband, they didn't see how I could survive on the money I made from writing. Had I asked, they would have been glad to help, but after college, it was understood—it was a point of pride—that I would live on what I earned.

I was surprised by how ferociously the women in my consciousness-raising group tore into their families as vectors of oppression. I didn't want to criticize my parents. I didn't feel comfortable enough with the other women in the group: discontented graduate students, discontented wives of discontented graduate students, a social worker, and one overwhelmed single mother whom we simultaneously admired, envied, and pitied.

Once, I heard a woman compare her consciousness-raising group to having all the lights turned on in a dark house, illuminating every corner. I'm not sure why mine wasn't like that, why the light sputtered and stayed dim. Maybe it was my fault. Maybe I was, and still am, uncomfortable in groups. Maybe I wanted to be part of a movement without belonging to a group. I thought of myself (and still think of myself) as a feminist, but those meetings always made me feel awkward and self-conscious. My leg or arm would fall asleep—mostly we sat on the floor—and everyone watched me try to restore the circulation, watched me pay for my silence and stiffness.

The pretty one, the neurotic one, the responsible mom, the resentful wife, they all seemed to be crawling back into the cocoon of their familiar, comfortable roles even as they tried to emerge as their bright new butterfly selves. The attractive and optimistic dominated the messy, insecure, and bewildered. And who was I? The lonely graduate student failing out of school, suffering from the pathetic delusion that she was a writer.

What I should have realized was that my being a writer was not unrelated to my discomfort in the group. The alienation, the sense of being on the outside looking in, the fear that I was seeing more than I probably should have, the habit of ceaseless observation, of note-taking without notes—it had become part of my work, of my job description, and, more importantly, of who I was and who I was trying to be: a person on whom nothing was wasted.

When my novel was accepted, the women congratulated and hugged me, but only a few of those hugs felt wholehearted. They weren't all that happy for me. They didn't like me all that much. That distance, that disapproval—it wasn't supposed to happen. We were one another's long-lost, newly discovered sisters. Only one—the wife of a graduate student—became a friend. She was not (I should say) the friend whose husband I was sleeping with because he played me Bob Dylan singing "I'll Keep It with Mine."

Maybe I was uneasy about the intensity of the group's rage at men. Sure, I was still angry at the high school senior I made out with at a party, in an upstairs bedroom because it seemed less stressful than being downstairs with the older kids, and who, on Monday, told the whole school that I was a slut. Sure, I was angry at the male professor I admired who mused about how *interesting* it was that female students were never at the top or the bottom of the class but always dead (he said *dead*) in the middle. Sure, I was angry at the publisher who put me in my place with the very first words of our first conversation; angry at my husband for his soporific lectures about why he was always right; angry at the older writer who told me that, in his day, men didn't publish novels until they were over forty and women not until they looked like Eudora Welty. Sure, I was angry at the Kirkland Street flashers who, with their innocent penises and guilty faces, helped convince me that the world was a hostile and dangerous place. Angry at the men who, I had recently come to understand, ran the world and had relegated me—without even knowing me!—to second-class status. But I was confused by the fact that I could be angry at men and still like and need them, that I could still respect and love them. I was afraid to ask the group about this contradiction without seeming traitorous and weak.

My mother navigated the male world of medicine and had close women friends all her life. When she died, in her late eighties, she was survived by a circle of girlfriends from childhood. But she was very much in my father's shadow. She seemed to like it there. And she certainly liked male attention. After my father died, her two best friends were men: a gay fashion-world superstar CEO and a married state trooper who looked like a '70s porn star. She was cheerful most of the time, but she really lit up around them.

When books about feminism began to appear in the 1970s, my favorite was the *SCUM Manifesto*, by Valerie Solanas, better known as the woman who shot Andy Warhol than as the funny, original writer she was. At one point she says that the only way for men to truly rehabilitate themselves would be for them to sit around in groups and repeat over and over, "I am a lowly abject turd."

I read this passage aloud to my women's group. No one laughed. I think I must have been seeking the special loneliness of being the only person who thinks that something is funny.

No one was laughing much. Tales of misery and disappointment emerged as our meetings devolved into something closer to therapy sessions. Women complained about their boring, stubborn, lazy, stingy, mean, bossy, entitled husbands. One woman asked us what we thought it meant that her husband wouldn't stop singing, "*If you can't be with the one you love, love the one you're with.*" Someone told her that she already knew what it meant, and then our hostess said, "Let's have dinner!"

Perhaps the problem was that I was lying to the group. I didn't want to admit how unhappy and restless I was, at least not before I'd admitted it to myself. I pretended to like my life. I added my (relatively) minor complaints—my husband ogled other women in a gross performative way intended to make me feel jealous and dissatisfied with my body. He often talked to me as if I were a disobedient, not-very-bright five-year-old trying her father's patience. But the women in my group defended him. A nice guy, really, they said. At least he does the dishes! And he's so good-looking!

One final possibility is that they were lying to me. For years I used to say that, after I left Cambridge, my husband slept with every woman in my consciousness-raising group. But, as I later learned, he only slept with one of them, or anyway, with one that I knew of. The woman whom I'd thought of as my friend. I didn't blame her. I deserved it. It was payback for what I'd done to my other friend whose boyfriend I had sex with because he played me Billie Holiday records. Both friendships ended. I've run into both women over the intervening years. We're sociable but distant. We don't talk about the past.

I told my parents, on the phone, that I was leaving my husband. They were delighted. My mother was practically giddy. They said they were sorry if it meant that I'd been unhappy, but it was okay, I'd made a mistake and now I could start over. I think they hoped that this time I would come to my senses and marry a neurosurgeon.

Both of them had gone through a lot to become doctors. Because of the restrictive quota on Jews in American universities, they'd gone to medical school in Glasgow until the war broke out, at which point the entire medical college relocated to the relative safety of Switzerland.

My mother came from a very large, very close Lower East Side family. She had never left home before. She always said that she became a doctor because none of the other women she knew were doing it, but I think it had something to do with the fact that when she was in high school, her sister, my aunt, fell ill with—and recovered from—tuberculosis, a dreaded and (at that time) potentially fatal disease.

In Glasgow, my mother couldn't get warm. She was miserably homesick until she met my father. They fell in love, which intensified the romance of their time abroad. In Lausanne, he translated for her. He spoke French and she didn't. On their way home, they traveled, protected by their American passports, by train across Nazi-occupied France and Franco's Spain. My mother was in constant fear until they reached Portugal, which had remained neutral in the war. She remembered falling asleep and waking to see the whitewashed Portuguese cottages rising up the hills on both sides of the tracks and thinking that she had died and awoken in heaven.

I never once saw my parents argue, which seems strange to me now. Was it because my father always got his way? Once, my mother told me that when she was supposed to meet my father on a street corner, and she first caught sight of him, her heart beat faster. After all that time. She said she hoped that someday I would feel that way about someone. I think she was telling me that she knew I would never feel that way about my husband, but that I might, someday, feel that about someone else.

My mother specialized in dermatology because she'd been told that dermatologists were never called out of bed for an emergency in the middle of the night. My father became a pathologist because he liked the culture of the autopsy room more than seeing live patients.

They were kind and decent and loving but also short-sighted. They were certain that medicine was the only meaningful work you could do. Having come of age during the Great Depression, they believed in security, safety, tradition. After I told them that I wanted to write, they kept telling me about doctors who were writers *in their spare time.* They had me at Chekhov and William Carlos Williams but lost me at Somerset Maugham.

They'd never liked my husband. They didn't care that he'd gone to Harvard. They said that they hadn't raised me to be patronized by an arrogant little shit. (In fact he was very tall.)

But they'd been relieved when we got married because we'd been living together. They hadn't gotten the memo about the new sexual freedom. They wanted a daughter independent enough not to be patronized by a man, but not liberated enough to have sex with him without being married. They embodied another example of what we called "the contradictions."

• • •

Quite a few of those "contradictions" had to do with sex. In that era of so-called sexual liberation, it was illegal in Massachusetts, until the early 1970s, to prescribe birth control to an unmarried woman. In college, I'd lied to get the pill. I'd made sure the doctor in Boston knew that I was a doctor's daughter. He had family photos around his office, a wife and a son and a daughter. I hoped he would see some version of his daughter in me and at least pretend to believe that I was married. He wouldn't want his daughter getting pregnant out of wedlock. Abortion was then a serious crime, as it would be for several more years. When my best friend in high school got pregnant, she'd had to go to Puerto Rico for an abortion, accompanied by her bewildered immigrant parents.

None of us were certain about what sex meant or didn't. Was it recreation or a commitment? How did you keep the heart from being confused by the body? And what did any of it have to do with love, whatever *that* was? You slept with people you met at a dinner party, with fellow guests staying with mutual friends. A friend brought home a guy who lived in a cave and whom she'd picked up at a swap meet in Orlando.

You didn't expect sex to be more than it was. It could be transcendent. Or not. You pretended to have no expectations, even when you did. Sometimes you had sex with someone because it seemed less complicated than saying no, though you knew that the person would have been perfectly gracious if you refused. There were frequent misunderstandings. Possessiveness and jealousy were embarrassingly old-fashioned. Monogamy was slated to be smashed without anyone's heart getting broken, so why were Janis Joplin and Joni Mitchell singing about heartbreak?

"Taking off our clothes," writes Jenny Diski, "was an important part of the project of undoing the constraints we believed our elders to have been immobilized by. We stripped conscientiously in front of each other and made nothing of it. Sex was written about and acted out in private and public with enthusiasm in the name of sexual revolution. The idea was to have fun, because having fun with our bodies was a completely new way of being with our peers."

Sex was a political act, part of being free. I can't remember ever hearing the tone I sometimes hear now when women describe their relationship to hookup culture: a mixture of sexual boasting and Puritan self-loathing. We were *supposed to* have control over our own sexuality. No one was *supposed to* make us feel guilty about it. We were not *supposed to* notice the gap between what we were supposed to feel and what we felt. How often I've written *supposed to* in a passage about freedom.

In that window between the availability of the pill and AIDS, as long as you had birth control and STD protection—and sometimes even if you didn't—you could have sex with people just to see what it was like. A plague of sexually transmitted crab lice spread through a group of my friends in New York, revealing a web of secret connections.

This is not a boast about how young and hot we were. If youth was a prerequisite, hotness rarely was. It was secondary to enthusiasm, curiosity, and desire. You learned that sex could be better than drugs, better than the best drug. Alternately, it could seem like a truly weird thing for people to do.

On the day before my wedding, my husband-to-be and I and his best friend—his best man—spent the afternoon in a Manhattan theater watching the Andy Warhol/Paul Morrissey film *Chelsea Girls.* When my husband-to-be went to buy popcorn, his friend and I made out, and when he returned, his friend and I held hands in the dark. I told myself it meant nothing. We'd simply been cutting the boredom of a three-and-a-half-hour black-and-white film in which nothing happens except Brigid Berlin shoots herself up, in the ass, with speed. Did my husband suspect what his friend and I had done? I never knew, but later I remembered that afternoon with guilt when I read Elizabeth Bowen's novel *The Death of the Heart.* The flash of a cigarette lighter, in a cinema, reveals that young Portia's beloved, a hustler named Eddie, is holding hands with the woman on his other side.

I'd spent my first night in San Francisco with that same friend of my husband's, his former best man. He had moved out West after college to work at a tech firm. I'd asked the guys who'd driven me to California to drop me off at his house.

After that night together in San Francisco, my husband's best friend was surprised that I was leaving to go stay with Henry and Grace, just as I was surprised that he'd thought I'd traveled across the country to live with him. The conversation that clarified things was painfully awkward, as such conversations always were, despite how casually and glibly we had learned to talk about freedom and sex and desire, despite how we'd learned to pretend that our plans and intentions were the result of passing impulses or crossed signals.

The wedding had been held in my parents' house in Brooklyn. It wasn't much of a party. My mother did all the cooking herself. Her cooking had declined since she discovered the potential of the stand-alone freezer and decided that everything could be improved by being frozen. She liked the challenge and the freeze-ahead possibilities of preparing large amounts of food for large groups of people.

My parents were uncomfortable with the newlyweds having their first state-sanctioned sex in their house, so we spent our wedding night in a tourist hotel near Times Square. We watched TV and fell asleep. I think we both knew that we had made a mistake.

The measure of the distance between the life my parents imagined for me and the life I went on to lead was their wedding present: an enormous set of Royal Copenhagen china in the Brown Iris pattern, soup tureens and gravy boats, cups and saucers with gilded edges, perfect for the damask-tablecloth-and-napkin dinners for twelve that I would serve when I was a doctor married to a doctor. The dishes and dinners were symbols of my parents' own ascent from the working class to the upper middle class, a process that I would reverse in my downward shift from an Ivy League student, schooled for success, to a boho writer collecting food stamps in San Francisco.

Against all odds, I still have the dishes, the entire set, after many moves and losses. My mother kept them for decades, and now they're neatly stacked in a 1930s toothpaste-green metal cabinet just outside my kitchen. The Brown Iris pattern is beautiful, but in fifty years, I have used the dishes exactly once, at a very large dinner for an elegant friend who, I knew, would like his birthday cake served on china thin enough to see through. The dishes are way too delicate to survive the dishwasher, and if all that gold trim accidentally took a turn in the microwave, it could blow all the wiring in the house. If a teacup broke, it would make me miss my parents. These days, when I walk past the dishes, I pretend not to see them, and sometimes I feel that the irises are pretending not to see me.

On my second night in San Francisco, Henry and Grace asked me to go out and buy avocados at the twenty-four-hour supermarket a few blocks down the hill. Everyone wanted guacamole. Everyone was high. It was midnight. As a guest, newly arrived, I couldn't say, No, I'm sorry, I'm too scared.

Henry and Grace's friends were kind and funny and welcoming, and I didn't want to start my new life by describing the problems I'd brought along from my old one.

I walked the two deserted blocks to the store. It was shocking, not being afraid. Just moving forward at an ordinary speed through the cool August night felt like being pitched into a tub of ice water, except that I liked it. I felt like a woman playing the part of a woman in a film who goes out alone in the dark. I tried not to think how many films begin with that woman chased, barefoot and screaming, through a forest. I tried not to think about the things in films that could happen in real life.

In Cala Foods, a heavenly fluorescent radiance shone down on the gorgeous California produce, the perfect artichokes, the museum-quality avocados. The only other customers were a half dozen drag queens, in full beards, feather boas, chest hair, and satin gowns. They skittered like butterflies, only louder, maximizing the drama of stuffing family-sized bags of candy corn into their shopping baskets.

I believed that they were angels sent from heaven to announce—cue the trumpets—that I had traded the darkness for the light. Whoever these marvelous creatures were, they were not like anyone in the Harvard English department. I felt dazzled, like Dorothy leaving black-and-white Kansas for a world redecorated in the rainbow pastels of a children's breakfast cereal.

What were the odds of finding a perfectly ripe avocado? In Cambridge, zero. In San Francisco, apparently one hundred percent. I got tortilla chips, in case Henry and Grace didn't have any. I was just beginning to remember how it felt to be normal, not to be scared. The kid at the counter could hardly ring up my purchases, he was so enraptured by the glitter and gowns and wigs.

Back at the apartment, I learned that my fellow shoppers were celebrities: the Cockettes! A wildly original theater group, led by the inspired Hibiscus, the troupe performed in the Nocturnal Dream Show at the Pagoda Palace Theater, staging their loopy, hilarious plays, including *Tinsel Tarts in a Hot Coma!* They'd made a wonderful film, *Tricia's Wedding*, about Nixon's daughter's White House moment of glory, a merry drag ball that descends into orgiastic violence when Eartha Kitt spikes the punch with LSD.

A random Cockettes sighting on my first night in San Francisco! Everyone agreed that it was a good sign. The guacamole was delicious, and my hosts thanked me for remembering to buy chips.

By the time I'd taken to my bed, that first year in graduate school, my husband must have begun to realize that he was about to wind up with a mental patient on his hands. To his credit, he agreed to go wherever I wanted, to do anything that might help me feel less stranded and anxious, to see if there was somewhere else he could temporarily use his graduate fellowship.

I suggested that we go to whatever approved science institute was geographically farthest from Cambridge, Massachusetts. We spun the globe. When it stopped, my finger was on Bombay, where there was such an institute and whose director wrote to say that they would be delighted to host a visiting Harvard graduate student.

At that time, you could get a surprisingly inexpensive around-the-world plane ticket from Pan Am that allowed you to stop off in as many places as you wanted, as long as you kept going in one general direction. We traveled via San Francisco, then Hawaii, Taiwan, Thailand.

Nearly everywhere we went—Honolulu, Bangkok—the hotels were full of US servicemen on leave from Vietnam, on holiday for R and R, rest and relaxation. Always they had local women with them, always young and beautiful. Always they sat around in groups, two soldiers and two women drinking beers or cocktails or iced coffee. Always the women looked deadly bored, chatting with each other or inspecting their nails or staring into the middle distance while the men talked to their buddies. What were they saying? The men and women never seemed to speak to one another. I tried not to stare. I was ashamed of what these soldiers and their rented girlfriends said about the US, about Americans in Asia.

I told myself that I wasn't part of it, I wasn't implicated, but

I knew that I was. Silk-screening posters and going to antiwar demonstrations hadn't been enough. I knew, even then, that the soldiers weren't monsters. They didn't seem glad to be in Asia. Most of them looked like homesick kids. They'd fallen into the hopper of the war machine and hadn't had the means or the connections to escape before it ground them up and spat them out in the jungle.

After a week or so in a cheap hotel in Bombay, my husband and I rented a plain unfurnished apartment in a newly built concrete apartment house in Colaba, in South Bombay, directly above a fishing village. Our terrace looked out onto the Arabian Sea, and at night the warm ocean breeze carried the music of the fishermen playing the harmonium and singing. Neighbors warned us to be sure and pin our laundry to the line lest our socks be stolen by the enormous seabirds swooping in from the shore.

We had a bed, a gas ring to cook on, a rented refrigerator, and two long rectangular mats for couches. I loved the apartment, and I loved living there from the minute I arrived. I remembered one of the medieval philosophers saying that you could narrow your distance from God by traveling, and that—or something like that—was what I believed had happened.

A friend had told me a fable about a vegetarian holy man who tells his vegetarian disciple to take a chicken and go someplace where no one sees, and kill the chicken, and bring it back, and they'll cook it. The disciple leaves but brings the bird back unharmed. He tells his master that he couldn't kill it. Wherever he went, wherever he thought that no one would see him, he'd think: The chicken sees.

The chicken sees. My friend said that the story meant that God sees, no matter where you go. I thought it meant that *you* would see, that you would see yourself killing the chicken, that you would never stop seeing yourself no matter where you went. So there was no point going anywhere and trying to kill the chicken because you would always be the same person failing to kill the same chicken.

In India, I learned that wasn't true. The chicken doesn't see very well, and in a different place, you can feel like a different person. In Bombay, I seemed to have become someone who loved her daily life. The poverty I saw around me was as bad as I'd imagined—worse. But I told myself that the suffering would continue to exist whether or not I was there to see it, and that my presence wouldn't change it, unless you counted the tiny bit of fellowship money we were putting into the economy.

The days were long, in a good way, and I had them to myself. I learned my way around the city by riding the two-decker public buses, twisting up the spiral staircase to the upper deck as the driver tromped on the gas, riding to the end of the line, then getting off, getting on, paying again, and riding back.

On weekends we watched Bollywood films in air-conditioned theaters. It was very hot, and Sunday matinees were crowded with people cooling off.

Once, waiting for a movie theater to open, I fainted from the heat. I'd been sitting on some shallow steps in front of the theater, and when I stood, everything seemed to have been covered with tiny mirrors, all glittering in the sun. I felt suddenly sleepy, more exhausted than I'd ever been, and then I was lying on the sidewalk, looking up at a small crowd of helpful, concerned Indians, all offering advice.

"I have dysentery," I explained, though I didn't, and then I blacked out again.

Back in my apartment, I lay in bed, talking quietly to friends on the other side of the world as if they were in the room. I don't know why my husband didn't call a doctor. I think I told him not to. The next day I was fine.

I got a borrower's card for the Bombay University Library, with its leaded windows and spires and gray stone turrets evoking some homesick colonist's heat-blurred memory of Oxford. Its quadrangles were landscaped with mango and coconut palms, and the humid air glistened with swarms of tiny bugs. The library had an extensive collection of Asian and European literature in translation, but nothing written after Partition, in 1947. Though I didn't quite realize it at the time, it was immensely helpful to me to be forcibly separated from contemporary fiction. It silenced the unhelpful voice in my head that suggested I might want to write like Richard Brautigan.

I borrowed and read the novels—Austen, Cervantes, *Little Dorrit*, Proust—that I'd skimmed or pretended to read in college. Reading was joyous in a way that it hadn't been since high school, since the summer happiness of returning from the public library with an armload of books, settling into the hammock on the side porch, *becoming* Jane Eyre or David Copperfield, forgetting who and where I was.

I shopped for food in the Colaba market, which was steps from my house and where the fisherwomen got to know me and yelled and waved me over when I walked in. My neighbors said this was because they charged me double, but I didn't care. I befriended my neighbors and their kids, who wanted to practice their English, and the lonely Russian wife of an Indian mathematician. Sometimes, on Sunday afternoons, we went to a kind of salon at the decaying Malabar Hill mansion of a lecherous Polish octogenarian, a former disciple and friend of Gandhi's, who asked if my husband and I would be willing to tell him about our sex lives. We weren't. We wouldn't have had much to say.

I was never lonely. Sometimes, in the mornings, I'd go for coffee to the Sunrise Café, where hippie travelers waited around to be hired as extras in Bollywood films, playing Western tourists sunning themselves on Juhu Beach. I invited the interesting ones home for dinner: the red-haired Hungarian who'd escaped the Russians on the back of his uncle's motorcycle; the American musician studying the sitar and his handsome, bisexual Swiss boyfriend; the Midwestern guy I secretly suspected of working for the CIA and who confessed that he was lonely because everyone suspected him of working for the CIA. There was a small shoe store in the business district where Westerners went to change money illegally but at a favorable rate and to buy the hashish we broke into crumbs and smoked in funnel-shaped clay pipes.

From time to time, I'd spend a few hours at the air-conditioned library at my husband's institute, idly flirting with the visiting scientists and reading, in the *International Herald Tribune*, about the search for the Manson family, about the Weathermen's townhouse explosion, about the trial of Bobby Seale. For the moment all that seemed far away, though I knew I was closer to Vietnam than I'd been at home.

I began to write—in longhand, in a notebook—the steadily lengthening short story that would become my first novel. A tale within a tale within a tale within a tale set in eighteenth-century Poland, *Judah the Pious* owed a lot to Gabriel García Márquez and to Isak Dinesen, who was still popular then.

Isak Dinesen, whose real name was Karen Blixen, was a Danish aristocrat. Near the end of her life, she visited New York and, onstage, recited one of her long stories from memory. Ravaged by the venereal disease she'd caught from her husband, a Danish baron, she could only eat oysters and champagne. In her last photos she looks like a skull with glowing coals for eyes. If fewer people read Dinesen now, perhaps it's because of our uneasy response to *Out of Africa*, a cringey book-length love song to her colonial African idyll, or maybe because her *Gothic Tales* have come to seem a little precious.

Here's a Dinesen passage I liked at the time, this one about sex, from her story "The Roads Round Pisa." A young man, Count Augustus, is talking with a young woman who has been traveling disguised as a boy.

> "Now God," she said, "when he created Adam and Eve . . . arranged it so that man takes, in these matters, the part of the guest, and woman that of a hostess. Therefore man takes love lightly, for the honor and dignity of his house is not involved therein. And you can also, surely, be a guest to many people to whom you would never want to be host. Now tell me, Count, what does a guest want?"
>
> "I believe," said Augustus . . . "that if we do, as I think we ought to here, leave out the crude guest, who comes to be regaled, takes what he can get and goes away, a guest wants first of all to be diverted, to get out of his daily monotony or worry. Secondly the decent guest wants to shine, to expand himself and impress his own personality upon his surroundings. And thirdly, perhaps, he wants to find some justification for his existence altogether. But since you put it so charmingly, Signora, please tell me now: What does a hostess want?"
>
> "The hostess," said the young lady, "wants to be thanked."

The hostess wants to be thanked! How hopelessly retro, how coy! What if the hostess wants to enjoy the visit? What if the hostess wants to be treated as an equal? Was Karen Blixen *thankful* for the gift of syphilis? The passage has not aged well. The fact that I found it enchanting—what a lyrical and romantic way of writing about sex!—makes me despair of ever fully understanding the person I was then.

What I took from Dinesen and García Márquez were certain conventions of storytelling: stories within stories, plot turns, disguised characters revealing their true identities, an interest in magic, and an idealization of a mythical past. You can spot the influences in the first sentence of my novel. "Legend has it that the heavenly gatekeeper actually raised his arms and danced down the steps of his golden watchtower to greet the Rabbi Eliezer of Rimanov; his passage was obstructed by the small angels who had had to climb up for a better view of the newcomer."

It wasn't a book that I would write today. To be honest, it wasn't a book that I would read today, when I have limited patience with certain sorts of magical realism. But at that point it didn't matter what kind of book I was writing in that apartment on the Arabian Sea. I was doing it for fun, to entertain myself. Writing was pure happiness. No one was watching me write or reading over my shoulder. I didn't know and I didn't care if anyone would ever read my work or if it would ever be published. I wasn't trying to say anything. I wasn't trying to change anything. I was just telling a story.

Maybe I'd needed to be that far away from home. Maybe I'd needed to be somewhere warm. Maybe I'd needed to be in a place where I couldn't get any books written after the year I was born.

I let the stories within stories spin themselves out. I included historical details that I remembered from a book on Jewish magic and superstition, and I added heavily disguised versions of events from my life. I felt guided. I felt as if I were taking dictation, as if I were in a state of grace.

In *Loitering with Intent,* one of my favorite books, Muriel Spark's narrator describes writing her first novel. Writing "took up the sweetest part of my mind and the rarest part of my imagination; it was like being in love and better."

It was like being in love and better.

At the end of the academic year, we left Bombay and traveled—much of it overland—back to Europe and then the US. In Cambridge, I'd stopped leaving the house, but now it turned out that I could circumnavigate Afghanistan by bus, the only woman not veiled from head to toe except for a rectangle of mesh over her eyes.

I made the twelve-hour journey from Kabul north to Mazar-i-Sharif to see the great Blue Mosque. The landscape changed and changed again: green hills planted with flowering fruit trees, red rock canyons, deserts rolling toward rugged mountains covered with snow in April. I developed an instant crush on the French photographer who got off the bus in the middle of nowhere. In Mazar, at sundown, a flock of white pigeons circled the blue-tiled mosque that sat in the center of a garden like a turquoise block of ice, while the local men, each holding a pink or yellow rose, walked around the structure, talking softly.

In Kabul, I used to spend hours in a tea shop watching people pass by. The tall Pathan men, made taller by their turbans, with their antique muskets slung across their chests. The bearded, round-faced Tajiks who could have ridden their donkeys, side-saddle, out of a Mughal miniature. Even now, the smell of lamb sizzling over coals takes me back, half a century, to the kebab stands on every corner. At least once a day, the Afghan kid who worked for our hotel, bringing soda and food to Westerners too stoned to leave their rooms, asked if he could come in and sit on the edge of the bed and tell us, always as if for the first time, that he was a Shiite Muslim, a good Muslim, and that Sunnis were bad Muslims.

In Herat, I got so sick that the hotel owner became alarmed and kept sending me free cans of ginger ale. I didn't feel well enough to make the arduous trip to see the giant standing sixth-century stone Buddhas at Bamiyan. I told myself that I'd go there the next time I returned. In 2001, the statues were blown up by the Taliban. Much about that world is likely gone or changed beyond recognition after decades of war. But sometimes I still dream that I'm in Kabul, and that it looks the same. I dream that I'm standing at the bus station by the river, across from a little mosque that resembles an Eastern Orthodox church.

After the dirt roads and rubble of Kabul, after the women whose silky chadors streamed after them as they hurried down the street, after the turbaned men squatting in doorways, after the boys selling chickens in crates and crickets in hand-woven cages, Tehran seemed like Paris. People spoke French. Shopkeepers were delighted to learn that, like them, I was Jewish. We stayed at a hotel recommended by the more prosperous hippie travelers. In the breakfast room I met two sketchy American guys, "oceanographers" who had been doing research in a series of landlocked countries.

I spent an entire day in the covered bazaar. I wanted to buy rugs and spices and flowers and find an apartment and live there.

The next day I walked into a Pan Am office to change my airline ticket so I could stay for a few days longer. On the coffee table was the *Herald Tribune* with the photo of the panic-stricken girl crouched, screaming, on the ground—and an article about

the killings at Kent State. Not far from the airline office someone had set up a piece of protest street art: a dummy in a striped
prison uniform, blindfolded and tied to a chair. A sign across its
chest said something in Persian, and, in English, "Savak." That
was the shah's secret police force, which was still very much in
power. Some brave person had assembled the piece and installed
it in that public place.

I missed my family and friends, but I didn't want to go
home. During a stopover in London, we went to see the Beatles film *Let It Be*. I sobbed all the way through it. My husband
moved to another row.

How cold and rainy London seemed, how dull and bleak
the colors. I couldn't stop thinking about the Blue Mosque at
Mazar-i-Sharif, about the fisherwomen calling my name in the
Colaba market, about some women I'd seen in South India, car-
rying shiny brass pots on their heads, each wearing a bright,
different-colored sari, walking in single file along the top of
an emerald green berm. I missed the sultry humidity and the
fields, after the monsoon, along the road to the ruins at Sarnath,
outside Benares. I kept thinking about the tombs of the Muslim
saints in New Delhi's Lodi Gardens, lush even in the dry season, covered by a twittering canopy of bright green parakeets.
I missed Feroze, the sweet-natured high school kid who'd lived
next door to us in Bombay, who spoke perfect English, though
he insisted that he didn't, who was religious and whose favorite
subject was the different Muslim holidays.

I knew that I was traveling in the wrong direction, but that
was what my plane ticket said I had to do.

Almost as soon as I got back to Cambridge, the phobias flared up again, like a recurrent fever. I'd been able to cross the desert from Herat to Kandahar, travel over the mountains from Kabul to Mazar, but back in Cambridge, I couldn't go to Julia Child's favorite supermarket.

Because I'd done so badly during my first year in graduate school, a kindly professor, Roger Rosenblatt, agreed to let me stay in school if I taught English C, Beginning Creative Writing, a course that no graduate student wanted to teach because it didn't interest them and wouldn't advance their careers.

I taught the class in my living room, which my students thought was cool. They never knew that it was because I couldn't leave the house. They were only a few years younger than I was. I didn't tell them that this was my first class, and they were too polite to ask. Many of them were talented writers, and several have made it their life's work.

Meanwhile I rewrote my novel. I started over, from scratch, typing this time, without looking at the longhand text I'd written in Bombay. I wanted to make it as hard as I could. I wasn't sure that I wanted to finish the book and send something so private and personal out into the world for strangers to judge and despise or ignore. When I'd fixed everything I knew how to fix, done everything I knew how to do, I showed it to a former teacher, Monroe Engel, who taught me how to line-edit: what to cut, reword, rearrange, the most useful and teachable skill.

Monroe sent the manuscript to his editor at Atheneum, Harry Ford. A few weeks later Harry called to say that he wanted to publish my novel. This was when editors could publish a book without channeling the marketing department.

I was standing in my kitchen when Harry called. I had to ask him to repeat who he was and what he wanted. First I didn't understand what he was saying; then I didn't believe it. I leaned against a wall and grabbed the back of a chair. I saw myself falling. I saw broken limbs, I saw crutches, I saw punishment for good fortune beyond anything I deserved.

Harry supposed I'd be wanting an advance.

"I guess so," I said. "Sure. How much?"

"How much would you like?"

"What do *you* think?"

"How about one thousand dollars?"

"That would be amazing," I said.

By now, it's a joke about how poorly first-time novelists were paid then, even by established publishers. A thousand dollars bought more than it does now, but you couldn't live on it for very long.

Still, that conversation changed everything. Being published didn't change what I did, which was write. But the phone call changed what I could *say* I did. What I could tell myself I did. I could say I was a writer. I could begin to think that it was true.

Harry said he would send me an edited manuscript and a contract. We would talk again soon.

After I hung up, and all that day, I was certain that, if I went out and crossed the street, I would be hit by a bus, despite the fact that no bus routes ran anywhere near my apartment. I kept thinking that would serve me right. But serve me right . . . for what?

And if I wasn't hit by a bus, what then? Another life streamed ahead of me like a moving sidewalk at the airport. All I had to do was step onto it and let it take me away from Cambridge, away from graduate school, away from my husband forever.

• • •

With Harry's help, I revised the novel. He sent my manuscript to a famously erudite poet he published. The poet sent me a ten-page letter on yellow legal paper, handwritten, listing all the mistakes I'd made in my stupid attempt to set a novel in eighteenth-century Eastern Europe. Each of his corrections threw me into a panic, but Harry told me I could ignore them. I'd written a novel, not a history.

I visited Harry in his office in the Chanin Building, the Art Deco skyscraper on the corner of 42nd Street and Lexington Avenue. He introduced me to the publisher, the head of his firm, a handsome, imposing, elegantly dressed older man. Every gesture, every point of his pocket handkerchief, signaled how sure of himself he was, how comfortable in his perfectly suntanned skin. I am tall, but he was taller.

He came around his desk to shake my hand. He looked down at me and smiled. I looked up at him and smiled back.

He said, "You didn't write this whole book all by yourself, did you?"

Just as that first fee negotiation with Harry has become, over time, a joke, so time has turned this incident into a funny story about the odious and demeaning things that men used to say to women.

It wasn't funny when it happened. I felt woozy with insult and rage, shocked that this stranger's first impulse had been to insult me just because he could. Just because I was young and female and he was publishing my novel, he couldn't resist cutting me down to the size he thought I should be. It wasn't humorous—or friendly. Something about his smug, reptilian smile reminded me of the flashers exposing themselves in their cars on Kirkland Street.

The worst part was that I heard myself answer "Yes, I did!" in the high-pitched, giggly, overly bright voice of a little girl.

The publisher laughed. The tension dissipated. I had done what was required.

Harry remained expressionless. He must have been used to it. I wasn't the only woman he published. Back in his office, he gave me, as consolation, a half dozen beautiful books (he'd designed them) by the poets he published: Mark Strand, Donald Justice, Mona Van Duyn, Philip Levine, W. S. Merwin.

Many years later, I used Harry's labyrinthine office, the long halls that led to the publisher's baronial suite, in a novel. I made the publishing firm more evil than I believe mine was or maybe just evil in a different way. I knew that Atheneum's parent company was Raytheon, which manufactured the missiles currently being deployed in Vietnam. As much as I wanted the war to end, despite the demonstrations I'd gone to, the posters I'd silk-screened, it never crossed my mind to refuse to be published by a firm owned by the American counterpart of IG Farben.

After my meeting with his boss, Harry took me to lunch at his favorite French restaurant, another event that took decades to find its way into a novel. I had a scary tolerance for drugs, but none for alcohol. I hadn't drunk anything since I'd gotten sick on gin punch, at a party my sophomore year of college.

I ordered a whisky sour, the only cocktail I knew. Sure, I'll have another. Harry was having a second martini. Over our meal—snails in garlic butter, a roast half chicken that the cocktails made a challenge to eat—Harry and I split a bottle of wine. When the waiter moved the table away from the banquette on which I was sitting, I stood up and fell over. Harry was the perfect gentleman. As he put me in a cab and gave the driver my parents' address, he acted as if this happened every day, and for all I knew it did.

The first time I left Cambridge for San Francisco was in August. My novel would be published in January. So I wasn't really hurtling into the abyss or stepping out into the unknown when—the morning after my friends sent me out to buy avocados and I saw the Cockettes at Cala Foods—I sent the chairman of my Harvard graduate school department a letter, regretfully informing him that I wouldn't be returning to school in September.

I was a writer. I had a job. Something I wanted to do. Something I loved doing. When my second novel appeared in the spring of 1974, a little more than a year after my first book, I'd be getting a fraction of a second advance, slightly smaller than the first.

I dropped the old-fashioned letter into an old-fashioned mailbox, and felt a vaguely familiar emotion that it took me a while to recognize as joy.

Henry and Grace had a beautiful bright apartment, on the second floor of a two-story wooden-frame house. An outside flight of wooden stairs led up to our door from the sidewalk. Our bedrooms had large windows looking down on Parnassus Avenue. Behind our backyard a lushly forested hill rose up to the Langley Porter Psychiatric Institute. I liked telling people that I lived on the grounds of a mental asylum, especially after I felt sane enough so that it seemed like a joke and not a disguised cry for help. A curtain of fuchsia blossoms with their pink and purple ballerina skirts, their dangling white legs and yellow pollen shoes, parachuted into our back garden.

Henry and Grace were glad to split the rent, and we established a congenial household. A couple and a single person living together can bring out everyone's best behavior. We survived on avocado sandwiches on San Francisco sourdough bread with mayo, black pepper, and alfalfa sprouts. On special occasions we ordered delicious plantains and roast chicken from the Ecuadorean bodega that accepted the food stamps that Henry took me to apply for at the FDA office as soon as I officially moved in.

Food and rent were cheaper then, and the lower cost of living gave people—by which I mean childless young white people—a freedom and mobility that we never had before and have never had since, except for the very rich. If you didn't like your apartment or your city, you could go somewhere else. Someone was always driving somewhere; someone always had a spare bedroom or a reasonably comfortable couch. You could write a book review, you could tend bar, you could be a waitress, work in a store, you could be somebody's studio assistant and pay the bills. And you could stay with friends as a *guest* for much longer than you could *couch surf* today. The confluence of cheap rent, youth, and transience meant that guests often stayed for absurd lengths of time, forever poisoning their relationship with the host. My friendship with Henry had barely survived the months he'd stayed with us in Cambridge. Later I would stay for months with filmmaker friends in a Soho loft, and another few months with friends in a farmhouse outside New Haven.

I talked to Henry and Grace about finding a place of my own. Friends who lived in communal houses in the Bay Area invited me to rent one of their extra rooms. But I remained at Henry and Grace's, which meant establishing the shallowest roots—no lease, no paperwork—that I could put down. I always knew that I would return to New York, where I had grown up, where my family and closest friends lived, and which I still thought of as home.

There were always plenty of people around the Parnassus Avenue apartment. Henry's college friends from Reed, Grace's childhood pals, and a group of artists, musicians, and inventors who had carved ingenious lofts and studios out of the Reno, a massive abandoned hotel south of Market Street. The hotel was built in the previous century for professional boxers and tunneled throughout with hollow shafts designed to give them a steady infusion of fresh air. The structure had been condemned by the city, but the ground floor was intact. The fire department let the artists remain in return for keeping the place together and ignored the fact that the residents were heating a fire trap with wood stoves. In 1979, the Reno was torched. But by then, the artists, who had seen the end coming, had stripped the structure of its old-growth redwood lumber and used it to construct new houses elsewhere.

Also among the regulars at Parnassus Avenue was an elderly retired pathologist, a charming Texan, more or less high-functioning despite his heroin habit. His filmmaker son, who'd gone to school with Henry, kept trying to make his dad quit using. It was almost a game, a drama that featured the son flushing the doctor's stash. We took turns accompanying the doctor to restaurant meals (he preferred Vietnamese) that he paid for and we couldn't have afforded. Our job was to get him home in a cab after he nodded off at the table. I felt that I had a gift for doing this because that was what Harry had done for me when I got drunk at our first publishing lunch.

I introduced a few of my college friends into the mix. Most had grown up in San Francisco and come home. Either they were running for local office, or working as radical lawyers, or living in Berkeley in loosely structured communes for semi-closeted gay alcoholics. Sometimes I went camping on the beach at Mendocino with the alcoholics, which was fun, except for the drunken drive home, weaving across the Golden Gate Bridge in a rusty panel truck with no seat belts.

Later, I would be reminded of the time I lived in California when I read Joan Didion's essay about the first time she lived in New York: "It never occurred to me that I was living a real life there. In my imagination I was always there for just another few months, just until Christmas or Easter or the first warm day in May." People live on a different calendar, she wrote, when they always have, in a drawer, a schedule of outgoing plane flights.

You form different relationships and make different decisions when you aren't planning on staying. You don't expect your new friendships to withstand the test of distance, and your love affairs, you tell yourself, need to last only until you have somewhere else to go.

In San Francisco, I was living on what remained of my book advance. Henry wrote science-fiction-themed pornography for a famous French publisher, famous for publishing Beckett, Burroughs, Henry Miller, and Nabokov—and for not paying his writers.

Grace worked in a dress shop in Ghirardelli Square. The store—Madame or Contessa or Principessa Something or Other—sold clingy Italian knitwear that looked dreadful on everyone regardless of age, shape, or physical beauty.

Grace was smart and acerbic and pretty in the pale, Pre-Raphaelite way that redheads cultivated then. I liked going out drinking with her after she got off work. Her idea of fun was to go to the singles bars on Union Street, the Black bars on Fillmore, or the hippie bars in the Haight and get men to buy us one cocktail apiece and finish it and thank them and leave. It was all about the hasty exit, about glimpsing that momentary flare of disappointment. We never got into trouble. It was Grace's feminist mini-payback, though she would never have called it that. She'd grown up in Oregon. She'd met Henry in Portland when he was at Reed. Even after a few drinks, she was an impeccable driver.

The first time I met Grace at the store where she worked, I was shocked by how much it looked like Ransohoff's, the sophisticated dress salon in *Vertigo*, Alfred Hitchcock's 1958 film. Scottie, a detective, has taken a woman named Judy to the shop to buy a suit. He hopes that the tailored dove-gray outfit will transform tough working girl Judy into her near double, his beloved ice queen, Madeleine Elster, who, he half believes, will return from the dead if he can only dress Judy in a replica of Madeleine's pencil skirt and nip-waisted jacket.

On leave from the police department, Scottie has been hired by wealthy Gavin Elster, whose wife, Madeleine, has been making entranced, ritualistic pilgrimages to a mission graveyard and to a museum. Scottie trails Madeleine and watches her throw herself into the bay. He saves her, then brings her to his

apartment to recover. After Madeleine dies in a shocking accident, he spots a young woman who looks just like her, except
that Judy is redheaded instead of blond, working class instead
of patrician. Scottie sets about transforming Judy into the dead
Madeleine. All it will take is the flawless blond chignon and the
magical gray suit from Ransohoff's, which is how they wind up
at the shop like the one where Grace worked.

I've watched the film over and over without ever tiring of
it, maybe because it always seems to be about something else.
Like all great art, it changes along with us, attaches itself to
one reading and another as time shows us what we overlooked
or what we were too young and inexperienced to understand.

When I was often angry at men, I believed that the film was
about necrophilia, about Sleeping Beauty, about men preferring
dead or unconscious women to living beings with minds of their
own. Then I decided that the film was about obsession, about
the ways in which Madeleine's pretend fixations are mirrored
by Scottie's real one. Then I decided that the film was about
social class, about men's aspirational longing for a certain kind
of chic, wealthy blonde. Then I decided that the film was about
the way that some people have a type, a face or body or character trait that's imprinted on them, an ideal they find or lose
early on and continue to look for, hopelessly and forever. Then I
decided that it was about the destructive effects of lying. Scottie
is being lied to, and he learns how to lie to himself in ways that
will prevent him from ever being happy.

In 1974, San Francisco looked to me very much like
it looked to Alfred Hitchcock and his cinematographer, Robert
Burks: sharp-edged, bright and ghostly, desperately romantic,
filtered through a dreamlike haze. The action is accompanied

by Bernard Herrmann's lavish, ominously propulsive score, the swells of music that mimic the rush of love, the five-note theme that rises, then falls on the descending half notes that follow.

I'd been to many of the places in the film: The Mission Dolores cemetery. The Legion of Honor, where Madeleine Elster spends hours gazing at the portrait of Carlotta Valdes. The Palace of Fine Arts. They were pilgrimage spots, like Kafka's grave, or Flaubert's house in Rouen, where my husband lectured me about Flaubert's perfectionism and his misogyny, and where I felt like Emma Bovary: in the wrong place, with the wrong husband, pining for the wrong men. Bored senseless.

When I remember San Francisco in 1974, the first images that come to mind are from *Vertigo*, and I have to remind myself that the city I lived in was not the one that Hitchcock filmed. During their first meeting, Scottie and Elster complain about how San Francisco has changed for the worse.

They should have seen it in the '70s. People like the Elsters still swanned in and out of the mansions on Russian Hill, but if they ventured down into the flatlands, they were in for a shock. The Summer of Love was over, and no one had swept up after the party. There were no more ecstatic be-ins in Golden Gate Park, the Grateful Dead were on perpetual tour, and the Diggers—with their guerrilla theater and free food and housing for all—had moved on. The Cockettes were the boldest reminder of how oxygenated the atmosphere used to be. Artists and writers were moving north to Marin County, and AIDS would soon scythe its way through the city, starting with the Castro.

The drug-addled hippie squalor that Didion found in the Haight and described in "Slouching Towards Bethlehem"—the mindless communal stupor, the toddlers tripping on acid—seemed paradisical compared to downtown San Francisco.

Nearly every corner had its resident meth heads, scratching themselves bloody. It had taken less than a decade for the city to change from *Hair* and *Jesus Christ Superstar* to *Mad Max* and *Panic in Needle Park.*

Richard Nixon was in the White House. The FBI was unstoppably determined to destroy the Black Panthers. Searching for the Zebra killer and Field Marshal Cinque, Bay Area cops routinely stopped and searched Black men at random.

It was harder to feel optimistic about a better future. Nothing seemed quite as sexy, as new, as fluid as it once did. Like the knitwear in the shop where Grace worked, the fashions of the '70s—the wide lapels and flowing sleeves and bell-bottoms— flattered no one.

Grace got me a job at the dress shop. I think she knew that it wouldn't work out, but she had a mischievous streak. She told me to wear my simplest and most expensive dress and to put on makeup.

I lasted less than a day. Grace's manager fired me for hiding in the changing room whenever a couple walked in. I was afraid that, like Scottie, the man would ask me to turn his female companion into the living replica of a dead woman. It was a fear I had in Cambridge, that something I saw in a movie could happen in real life.

Not long after I met Tony, on one of those late-night drives, we passed the building from which Madeleine swirls out past the doorman, across the courtyard and into her sleek scarab-green Jaguar.

Tony said, "The *Vertigo* building."

"I was just thinking that." I was thrilled that Tony knew. I tried to keep my voice level.

I didn't know much about Tony then, but I thought I understood why he might love the film. Like Scottie, he was an obsessive, the difference being that Tony was obsessed with ending a war and Scottie with a dead woman.

Vertigo. Gravity's Rainbow. The Sutro Baths. The Chi-Lites. Maybe our shared enthusiasms meant more to me than they should have. Maybe I was trying to convince myself that love was the sum you got when you totaled the list of *things* that the two of you liked.

Tony said, "Did you scream during that last scene?"

I said, "It terrifies me every time."

"Me too. All that horror I'd seen in Vietnam, the real horror, the real blood and the real death, and I'm scared shitless by the shadow of a nun in a movie."

We were nearing the Marina when he said, "How much do you . . . ?"

A damp wind rushed into the car. "How much do I what?"

"How much of the story do you know?"

"Which story?"

"Mine, obviously." He laughed. "Mine and Dan Ellsberg's. What other story is there?"

I said, "I know what everyone knows."

"In other words, nothing." He laughed again.

Don't, I thought. Don't even smile at me. Keep your eyes on the road.

I asked Henry and Grace about Tony. I called friends, but they'd gotten a little fuzzy about the details of the Pentagon Papers. Three years had passed since the release of the documents, one year since the Ellsberg-Russo trial. A lot had happened since then.

Like most people, I knew more about Ellsberg than about Tony. Ellsberg was the guy who actually stole the Pentagon

Papers, Tony the guy who talked him into leaking them, showed him how, and helped him do it.

A former marine, Ellsberg bought into the domino theory and into the Cold War rhetoric that framed the world as a battleground between good and evil, American democracy versus Soviet totalitarianism. He was haunted by Hiroshima, by thermonuclear war. He'd gone to work at RAND as a strategic analyst. He left for the Defense Department, then the State Department. In 1967, he returned to RAND.

Ellsberg was an idealist, a borderline fanatic of an essentially well-meaning kind. Determined to experience war, he volunteered on combat missions. In one photo he is holding a rifle, hiding in tall grasses. In another he's drinking from a coconut in a field while a Vietnamese woman walks behind him, with baskets on a pole across her shoulders.

In Vietnam, Ellsberg changed his mind about the war because of what he saw in combat and what he heard from the Vietnamese, who didn't care who won the war, just so long as it ended. He came to believe that the war was not just politically unwise but a crime against humanity.

Also Ellsberg was, in his youth, something of a womanizer, and all the prettiest girls were against the war. According to the documentary *The Most Dangerous Man in America*, Ellsberg's love affair with Patricia Marx, a progressive journalist and heiress whom he later married, initially ended because of their conflicting views on Vietnam.

Whatever suspicions Ellsberg harbored about American involvement in Southeast Asia were confirmed when he read the seven-thousand-page report that McNamara commissioned.

In *The Most Dangerous Man in America*, Ellsberg says, "I heard Congressman Pete McCloskey give a speech. He had come back from Asia and revealed information about the secret bombing of Laos. And here was a representative with the guts to use the word . . . *lies."*

Ellsberg pauses for a beat before he says *lies,* as if he still believes that the word has an explosive charge that might detonate on contact. Or maybe he's remembering a time when the word still had, or seemed to have, that much moral force and power.

I didn't mind taking a bus across town and spending the day at the public library to learn what I could about Tony. I loved the monumental Beaux Arts facade, interrupted halfway up by eight massive columns, the sweeping marble staircase that rose through a skylit atrium surrounded by a loggia lined with murals of land- and seascapes in the subtle colors of a Japanese print. I loved the clacking of typewriters, the smell of furniture polish and glue. I loved the long wooden tables in the main reading room beneath the pendant Art Deco chandeliers. I loved how hushed the room was, how overheated. In winter, it was the warmest place in San Francisco.

A helpful librarian showed me—not for the first time, sorry!—how to thread the microfilm viewer. Columns and advertisements flipped by, time ran backward, plays and movies closed and opened, sales ended and began, the cost of everything dropped as the pages turned from the present into the not-so-distant past.

I wanted to know who Tony was, what had happened to him. To get the chronology straight. I could have asked him, but I hesitated to rouse the tearful genie that certain subjects seemed to wake.

Born in 1936, Tony Russo grew up in southeastern Virginia, on the edge of the Great Dismal Swamp, a nature preserve once home to indigenous and formerly enslaved people.

A brainy, middle-class kid who played high school football, he knew he was a privileged white guy in a part of the South that wasn't officially desegregated until he was in his teens. *Brown v. Board of Education*, the Supreme Court ruling that outlawed segregation in public schools, was passed when he was eighteen. He was one of the young men who saw Kennedy as a leader whose call to action they wanted to follow. Ask not what your country can do for you but what you can do for your country.

Tony was a patriot. He believed in the Constitution, in the Bill of Rights, in democracy.

By the time he graduated with an engineering degree from Virginia Polytechnic Institute, the draft had become a problem. It can't be overstated how much the public outrage over the Vietnam War was fueled by the fact that middle-class white kids were being drafted, unlike today's "volunteer" military, culled from the poor and communities of color. If those populations made up a disproportionate fraction of our army in Vietnam, it was partly because guys like Tony, Henry, and my husband had the resources to avoid being drafted. They weren't cowards or traitors. They weren't about to risk their lives in a war that we shouldn't have been fighting.

In Boston, people passed around the contact information of a psychiatrist who, for $500, would see each patient a few times and write a letter stating that the patient was unfit for military service. That was why Henry had come to live with us—to see the antiwar shrink.

I don't think the doctor was lying. The men he saw *were* unfit for military service, if only because their privilege made them believe that they had a choice about what happened to them. It helped that the army was sensibly wary of young men determined not to join. Reluctant recruits could cause trouble, even endanger their fellow soldiers.

A friend who wore women's underwear and a hoop earring to his draft physical was quickly sent home. Whatever the draft board thought this signified, he had made something clear. Everyone who didn't go to Vietnam had a story, as did everyone who went.

Tony's career choice was influenced by his natural gift for science and math and by a calculation about which professions might keep him out of the military. He went from engineering school to NASA, where he worked in the space-capsule program and studied the absorption of radio waves by a hot flow field. Bored and restless, he enrolled in graduate school at Princeton. Some of his friends—foreign students—told him how disappointed they were in the US for continuing France's colonial war in Vietnam. It was the first time he'd heard anyone question a Kennedy policy, and their conversations made him begin to question the war.

In June 1964, he left Princeton for Santa Monica, to work in RAND's Cost Analysis Department. Tony's friends warned him not to take the job. Tony knew about RAND's role in perpetuating the war, to which he was becoming opposed. But at that time, it was believed that powerful institutions could be transformed *from within* by *infiltrating the establishment*.

"In retrospect," Tony wrote, "I think I felt that I could be a kind of anthropologist, observing the natives in the village of the Pentagon . . . The RAND Corporation was where the action was, covering all bases from the thermonuclear aspect of things to research in Vietnam. I had the naïve notion that, if reason could be brought to bear in a process that looked questionable to me, then perhaps some good could be done. I was caught up in the myth of working from within . . . My friends were . . . skeptical. I was alone in thinking the belly of the whale might be an interesting place to work."

Among the important contracts that RAND procured was one for gathering and analyzing intelligence on the commitment of the Vietnamese people, North and South. By providing information about the resources and the fighting spirit of both sides, RAND believed that it could help the Pentagon predict the likelihood of an American victory.

Tony went to Vietnam to take part in RAND's Motivation and Morale Study. He talked his way into the project. I think *his* motivation was curiosity. Who were the Vietnamese? Why were they fighting? What did we have in common? Had the North Vietnamese been brainwashed, or were they true believers? He wouldn't have gone if he hadn't already had doubts about what the US was doing. He was already, as he would say about Ellsberg, halfway out the door.

"Vietnam," Tony wrote, "taught me that the America that was in Vietnam was the opposite of the America I'd learned about in school. Our nation had not been founded, our Constitution had not been framed, to condone genocide. I wanted the American people to discover for themselves what I'd learned in Vietnam."

Only an idealist—or an egomaniac—would have imagined that an institution working for the Defense Department could be turned around by the force of his personal righteousness and charisma, by his dedication to truth and to the Constitution. What Tony learned was that a large conservative think tank with strong ties to the Defense Department was unlikely to be changed by a progressive employee. He learned a lesson about power, about what the powerful can do to the powerless, and about how reckless and cruel the powerful can be.

Another book that Tony and I talked about was Kurt Vonnegut's *Mother Night*, a World War II novel about a man who believes he is a double agent, transmitting coded communications to the Allies disguised as propaganda broadcasts for the Nazis. Ultimately, it turns out that there were no coded messages and that in fact he was only making propaganda broadcasts for the Nazis.

"We are what we pretend to be" is the novel's most quoted line. "So we must be careful about what we pretend to be."

Tony had told himself that he'd been working to change RAND from within, but he came to believe that he was responsible for what they'd done—guilty for not trying harder to stop it. He'd gone into the office, eaten lunch and shot the shit with colleagues who advised the military to step up the bombing campaign.

He'd worn the RAND name tag, he said, as if he was confessing to a crime. He'd worn it even after he was fired. He called it his badge of shame, his scarlet *A*. Whenever he mentioned it, he wept and his hand drifted to the center of his chest, where the badge had hung.

One night I asked him, "What did you do with the RAND name tag?"

"I threw it in the Pacific. Then I fished it out. What if a big swordfish ate it and someone found it and . . . you know the story. I thought about burying it in my yard in Santa Monica, but I was being watched. I could just imagine some FBI freaks digging up the lawn to find my name tag. Plus the garbage men are still going through my trash. So I can't get rid of it. It's somewhere in my apartment. I'm stuck with it forever. The plastic-coated mark of Cain on a cheesy metal chain."

Tony and Dan wanted to give the Pentagon Papers to an antiwar senator who could bring them to Congress, but Senators Fulbright and McGovern refused. Kissinger claimed to have no interest in the report because nothing could convey the *delicate complexity* of how policy decisions were made. Later he told Nixon that stealing the papers was an act of treason. He called Dan a madman and a pervert, "the most dangerous man in America."

Ellsberg showed the file to Neil Sheehan, at the *New York Times*, who went to Max Frankel, then the Washington bureau chief. Sheehan claimed to have gotten them from a confidential source. After consultation with their legal counsel, the *Times* decided to publish, though they knew the paper could be charged with espionage.

On June 13, 1971, the *New York Times* ran the story under a banner headline, "Vietnam Archive: Pentagon Study Traces 3 Decades of Growing US Involvement." The next day's follow-up article revealed that a consensus to bomb Vietnam developed before the 1964 election, even as Lyndon Johnson was promising American voters to end the war.

Nixon was furious, because he hated anything that made the government look bad and because the report upstaged the *really* important event of the day, his daughter Tricia's wedding. He was also afraid that the papers would release new information about his secret bombing of Cambodia and his efforts to sabotage the Vietnam peace talks. As Nixon's rage boiled over, Henry Kissinger distanced himself from Ellsberg, though he'd formerly befriended the younger man and enjoyed playing the avuncular foreign policy sage. Now he called Ellsberg an extremist radical so clinically insane that he had actually accused him—Henry Kissinger!—of murder.

"Destroy the son of a bitch" Nixon is reported to have said. "I don't care how you do it. You can't let the Jew steal the stuff and get away with it."

Attorney General John Mitchell sent the *Times* a telegram requesting that the paper stop publication—a threat that the publisher, Arthur Sulzberger, ignored. The Justice Department then asked a New York federal court to enjoin further publication, and when the *Times* refused, the judge issued a temporary restraining order.

Calling from pay phones under false names, Ellsberg contacted a former colleague, Ben Bagdikian, at the *Washington Post*. As excerpts appeared in the *Post*, Ellsberg and his wife, Pat, watched, on their motel TV, FBI agents and reporters surrounding their house in Cambridge.

The case made its way to the Supreme Court, where the justices ruled against the government in a landmark ruling upholding the First Amendment, a decision that would be cited, for decades, in cases defending free speech and the freedom of the press.

During a CBS News interview, filmed at a secret location while he was in hiding, Ellsberg said that it would hurt the American people to learn "that the men whom they gave so much respect and trust, as well as power, regarded them as contemptuously as they regarded our Vietnamese allies . . . We are the government. The lesson is that the people of this country can't afford to let the president run the country by himself."

On June 28, 1971, Ellsberg was arrested and released on $50,000 bail. As he left the courthouse, cameras snapped, flash bulbs popped, and Patricia Marx Ellsberg beamed up at him, rapt with adoration. What could be sexier than a husband whom Henry Kissinger had called the most dangerous man in America? The newspaper photos document Ellsberg's rapid transformation from a guilt-ridden policy analyst into a media darling.

After the story broke, Tony was easier to find than Ellsberg. Tony let himself be found. He wanted to be found. Whatever happened would be his penance for working at RAND.

Two FBI agents showed up in his driveway in LA and presented him with a subpoena to appear in court the following morning. The FBI also paid a call on Lynda Sinay, who'd let Tony and Dan use her copy machine. She was threatened with prosecution unless she testified, under oath.

After refusing to testify against Ellsberg, Tony was cited for contempt. Stays and continuances postponed his arrest, but on August 16, two months after the papers appeared in the *Times*, he surrendered at the courthouse and was taken to the Los Angeles County jail.

On that same day, in Los Angeles, Ellsberg pleaded not guilty to charges that could have sent him to prison for decades, a term that the judge, William Byrne, kept increasing until it topped out at 115 years for Ellsberg, 35 years for Tony.

On YouTube, there's a video clip of Tony recalling how happy he was when he thought he might be going to jail. He's sitting in a garden in front of a spray of bright greenery. The California sunlight is dappled and clear. Tony seems entirely at peace—radiant, beatific. His smile is steady and calm. Maybe he seems so tranquil and assured because he's revisiting the moment when he most fervently believed in what he was doing, the moment when he thought that they could change what had to be changed, and that the risks he was taking would prove to be worth it.

"One day there it was," he says, "in the newspapers. I felt so really . . . joyful . . . about this. I didn't care what they did to me. They could send me to jail. I could thumb my nose at them. There was no way they could undo the Pentagon Papers."

Undo the Pentagon Papers. He is talking about the documents as if they were a historical act rather than a stack of photocopies. He is describing a change in the political weather. You don't doubt him when he says *really joyful.*

He says, "The reason I felt such joy was that I was being true to myself. I remember thinking that people who worked solely for their paycheck or for personal power would never know that feeling."

In those days, people often talked about being true to themselves. But by 1974, what they meant by *truth* was beginning to shift from the collective to the individual, from political action to personal fulfillment. *My truth*, they began to say.

In prison, Tony was provoked by the guards, beaten for refusing to take the bait, and thrown into solitary confinement. When he complained about his eyeglasses being taken away and kicked the door of his cell, his wrists and ankles were tied behind his back, and he was forced to lie, trussed, on his stomach. When he refused to let the guards confiscate his journal, his toenail was torn half off, a bone was bruised, he got a bump on the back of his head. Hauled before a disciplinary committee, he was charged with agitating his fellow prisoners. He went on a hunger strike. When he was hospitalized for malnutrition, a sign on the door of his room prohibited visitors. Isolated from the other inmates, who had been forbidden to speak to him in the yard, he communicated with them by whispering into a ventilator pipe.

Six weeks after his arrest, Tony was released, then immediately rearrested on a manufactured disorderly conduct charge. The harassment continued. He never knew when he was going to be picked up by the police. He got used to checking his rearview mirror. During this time, he was put on leave from his job as an analyst at the Los Angeles County Probation Department.

"One day I looked down at myself in the prison," he said, "dressed in dirty pajamas and flip-flops, and it occurred to me that I was wearing what Vietnamese prisoners wore. My job had been to interview these guys, and now I had become one. And you know what I thought. I thought, I've been Vietnamized!"

I said, "That had been going on for a while."

"Good point," Tony said. I was pleased I'd said something about him that he agreed with. "Prison wasn't the first time that someone tried to kill me."

There was no way not to ask the next question, but I made myself wait. We were speeding past the water without looking at it, as if the ocean didn't matter, as if it were just a backdrop for the drama Tony was remembering.

"When was the first time?" I said.

"*Times*," he corrected.

"The first times."

"The first time was in Saigon. The week I handed in my defoliation report. I was sitting in an outdoor restaurant near the market, and I watched my car get bombed into a ball of flame shooting geysers of fire. My favorite shirt was on the back seat!"

"Who did it?"

"By that point? Not the Vietnamese. They knew I wasn't their enemy. I'd say it was friendly fire. Unfriendly fire. Whatever. *Friendly fire!* Another oxymoron. Like *military intelligence.*"

"Did you ever find out who it was?"

Tony shrugged. "I knew. You'd be in mortal danger if I told you. Why do you think they're still shining their headlights in my rearview mirror and throwing my garbage all over the alley."

I felt—suddenly, strangely—protective. I had never heard someone (outside the movies) say, Someone tried to kill me.

Tony hadn't been threatened because he robbed a bank or insulted someone or slept with somebody's wife. It was because he
had tried to tell the truth about a war.

How could I not be interested in a person who had done
that? How could I not listen and try to piece the fragments together? How could I not feel fortunate to be in that car, with a
hero, a rebel, speeding up and down the hills of San Francisco?
I had never met anyone like Tony, who had put so much on the
line and for such a good reason. I felt honored to be in that car,
always a little on edge, flattered, chosen, and unworthy.

At an early meeting of the so-called Special Investigations Unit, the team of fixers later known as "the plumbers," G. Gordon Liddy, White House aide Egil Krogh, David Young from Henry Kissinger's team, and former CIA officer Howard Hunt, discussed the best way to sabotage Daniel Ellsberg's growing popularity. By then, most Americans favored leaving Vietnam, so Ellsberg—unlike Edward Snowden and Chelsea Manning— wasn't considered a traitor except by a very few, among them Nixon and Kissinger, who were determined to bring him down.

Urged on by Liddy, with his shifty eyes and the mustache of a silent-movie villain, the men suggested slipping LSD into Ellsberg's soup at a dinner at which he was scheduled to receive an award. But the plan failed when Liddy's men couldn't get jobs on the waitstaff. Liddy is said to have decided that the likeliest source of dirt on Ellsberg—his embarrassing sexual kinks, obsessions, weaknesses, and anxieties—might lurk in the files of his psychiatrist, Dr. Lewis Fielding. The team agreed that Liddy and Hunt should hire a trusted unit headed by Bernard Barker to break into Fielding's office.

The five burglars—anti-Castro Cuban refugees with a passion for rooting out communists—approached their mission like jewel thieves in a caper film. Therapy notes might have been less glamorous and marketable than gems, but no matter. The Cubans preferred blackmailing an enemy of the state to fencing a diamond bracelet. To them, ransacking the office of a traitor's shrink was a patriotic act. Barker and his men prowled among the file cabinets and Kleenex boxes, the couches, kilim pillows, and carved totems of LA psychotherapy, only to discover that Dr. Fielding wasn't much of a note-taker.

The news of the Fielding break-in became public around the time that the Watergate scandal broke and deranged the nation's ideas about power, decency, and the integrity of our democracy. The government dropped its case against Ellsberg and Russo. That the Watergate burglars had practiced on Ellsberg's psychiatrist's office convinced US District Court Judge William Byrne that the connection between the two burglaries would make it impossible to conduct a fair trial. Also there was talk of Judge Byrne possibly heading to the FBI, an appointment that might have been compromised if the trial went badly.

The front-page *New York Times* headline May 12, 1973, reads "Pentagon Papers Charges Are Dismissed; Judge Byrne Frees Ellsberg and Russo, Assails 'Improper Government Conduct.'" On the same page, below and to the left, but also above the fold, is an article headlined "White House Says Attacks Will Continue in Cambodia."

By that winter, Ellsberg had become a star, courted by celebrities, while Tony was in San Francisco, writing a book, staying up all night, and driving around with me. It was doubly surprising that we were never stopped because the cops were on high alert, looking for Patty Hearst.

After I got home from the public library and was getting ready for my second date with Tony, if that's what it was, I spent so long in the bath that Henry, ordinarily patient, pounded on the door. I washed my hair and put on makeup. I took more care with my clothes and hair than I had before the poker game.

Just before Tony arrived, Grace pulled me into her bedroom and sat me on the edge of the bed and told me that yet another friend had said that Tony had been acting strangely. Not scary or unhinged, but also not . . . normal. He claimed that he was still being followed. After what had happened to him, no one could be sure he *wasn't* still under surveillance, but something about him seemed . . . well, no one knew what to call it. Also he'd had that intense response when Henry mentioned Patty Hearst.

I reminded Grace that he'd seemed fine at the poker game. Besides, he'd been through a lot. He'd been heroic. We needed to cut him some slack. I suppose I was convincing *myself* because, even during that first evening we'd gone out driving, he didn't seem entirely stable. The talking and the silence, the speeding and the tears, the sudden switches from being present to being somehow . . . *not there*—it was worrisome, or it would have been if I hadn't decided not to worry.

Grace said, "I'm just asking you to please be careful. With Tony. Maybe try not to get too involved."

I said, "What does *too involved* mean? I only met him last night."

"It means be careful," said Grace. "What did you two do, anyway?"

"We drove around."

"That's what you did? You drove around? Where?"

"We went to the Martha Washington."

"Classy," Grace said. "I rest my case."

"And the Sutro Baths."

"You went to the Sutro Baths at night? With a guy whom none of us know all that well, though I guess Henry claims that he does."

"I love the Sutro Baths. You know that."

"You *like* him!" said Grace. "God help us. You *like* Tony."

"So what? Is this high school?" I said.

I could see, from the window, Tony's car pulling up outside our house. For a second I couldn't breathe. I couldn't decide if I was happy that Tony was there or just glad that he wasn't *not* there. I grabbed my jacket and gave Grace a quick hug.

"Stay safe," she said.

"Oh, please," I said. "Honestly. Take it easy."

Tony rolled down the car windows. The cold, wet air smelled like San Francisco: moss, salt, eucalyptus, car exhaust. He pulled away from the curb and headed toward the avenues.

He said, "I had a good writing day today. Maybe because I met you."

Did he mean it? I wanted to think he did.

"How much have you got written?"

"Some," he said. "Early days. Maybe . . . two chapters . . . maybe one . . . it's hard to tell . . ."

It was the kind of evasive answer that I might give, that I *had* given, when I was asked about a work in progress—questions that seemed like jinxes. I'd heard writers speak at length about what they were writing, and I'd think: You should be more superstitious. Wait until you're a few commas away from being finished to talk about what you're doing. Clearly Tony hadn't reached the fiddling-with-commas stage.

He headed north and over the Golden Gate Bridge. He said, "This would be a beautiful drive if you didn't have to stay under the speed limit. The cops hang out at the end of the tunnel waiting to pull over convicted felons like myself. Me and the Zodiac Killer. Maybe I *am* the Zodiac Killer."

"Good idea," I said.

"What is?"

"Not speeding."

"Right. Please tell me you don't have weed with you or coke or . . ."

"Clean as a whistle," I said. "I have some weed back at Henry and Grace's. Do you want—?"

"No thanks. I could go to jail forever. But I always get a little high before I leave home. It improves my driving. You know what they say? Drunks run a lot of red lights and potheads stop on a lot of green ones."

"You run red lights," I said.

"Got it," he said. "I'll slow down. For your sake. I'll follow the letter of the law."

"Don't do it for my sake." I imagined other women, braver than I was, urging him to drive faster.

"I wasn't planning to," he said. "Drive any differently than I normally do."

Turning onto 18th Avenue, he said, "I can't remember what I told you about my book. I can't recall if I told you anything at all, which is strange, because it's what I'm doing. I'm writing about Vietnam, trying to tell my side of the story. I was going full steam, well, half steam, well, maybe a quarter steam, and then I got to the part about the Motivation and Morale project, and it stopped me. Stopped me cold. Writing was like chipping the letters from blocks of stone without a chisel. Like playing that test-your-strength game with the giant hammer at the county fair. To tell you the truth, that's where I'm at now, stopped by a washout roadblock. I'm trying to drive over it or blast through it and—"

"Do you know what the problem is?"

"I honestly have no idea."

"I don't know. I'm so sorry. One thing: You don't have to write chronologically. You can skip parts and then go back later." I hated how I sounded, like the writing teacher I was trying not to become—with Tony or anyone else. Within weeks of my first novel coming out, I'd been offered a job teaching writing at a small New England college, but the prospect seemed like getting married again and going back to school. Anyway, how could I help Tony? When I'd been revising my novel, he'd been trying to save lives. I'd written two novels and a few short stories, fiction dreamed up out of my head. How could I know what it took to describe interviewing torture victims?

"I heard that Dan got a half million dollars for a book he can't write. Do you happen to know if that's true?" He smiled the sheepish grin of someone caught trolling for publishing gossip.

"I don't know," I said. "I'm sorry I—"

Tony said, "It's one of the many things that Dan and I can't discuss."

"Like *what* things?" I asked.

"Like everything."

He wasn't going to say more. It was like a magic trick, the way he could disappear, his tortoise-like retreat, how far he could travel away from me without moving. I told myself that it wasn't personal. I thought of how often, how long, and by how many people he'd been interrogated. I wanted to hear about what he was trying to write. But I didn't ask.

I have always hesitated to ask people about subjects that they obviously don't want to talk about. It became a problem when I was writing interviews for editors who naturally wanted to know the one thing I hadn't been able to ask.

Tony said, "Do you have an agent?"

It was a question I'd come to dread because it so often led to the follow-up question: Was my agent taking on new clients? Tony wouldn't have a problem finding an agent. He was an anti-war hero.

"Sort of," I said. "He's a little weird. I got him through an old beatnik friend. All his other clients seem to be rogue New York City cops, Serpico types he meets under bridges."

"My agent's a wonderful person," he said. "She's Grace Paley's agent."

One of my teachers in college had read Grace Paley's stories aloud to us in class. It was the first time I understood that there was room, on the page, for a street-smart, funny, opinionated woman watching her kids in the playground, for women with strong political views, for lively *important* stories about childhood, marriage, friendship, motherhood, charming elderly Jews. I hadn't known that someone could write like that. I hadn't realized how much I'd longed to hear that tone, cadences I'd grown up with. For a while, I tried to imitate her style. The outwardly brittle but inwardly wan girls I wrote about in graduate school might have sounded like fragile, morose versions of Grace Paley's women, except that the women in her stories were *anything but* fragile and morose.

"I love her work," I said.

"So do I," said Tony. "She's the greatest."

That seemed even more significant than Tony and I both

loving the Delfonics, Thomas Pynchon, and the Sutro Baths. Maybe because Grace Paley's characters seemed to me so familial, maybe because her work was so close to my heart, I thought that Tony's liking her work must have meant he liked *me*.

Tony said, "And you also have an editor, right?"

"Also a wonderful person," I said. "Harry."

"Okay. Can I ask you a question? What does a book editor *do*? I've worked with magazine editors. They don't do all that much. But it must be different with books."

I said that I loved my editor. He published great poets. He cared about book design.

"But what does he *do*?"

"He replaces words with better words. He cuts repetitions and passages that slow things down. He says that they're only suggestions. The final decisions are up to me. The galleys come on these long sheets of shiny paper, you make corrections in the margins and—"

"That's not what I meant. I meant . . . when your book came out, when it was published . . . Was it *basically* the same book that you wrote?"

"What?" His question made no sense. "Sure. Yes. Why wouldn't it be?"

"And how would you feel if he changed every word without asking you, if he turned it into the opposite of what you'd written and published it with your name on the cover?"

"That couldn't happen. That *doesn't* happen."

"Worst-case scenario. Let's say it happened. What then?"

"I would have hated it. Obviously. Why do you ask?"

"Just curious," he said.

He drove to Sausalito and pulled into the lot of a restaurant on a dock overlooking the water. The Blue Fin, the Blue Marlin, the Clam Shack, the Oyster Bar. Let's call it the Great White Whale.

When I got out of the car, the wet cement felt, for a moment, as spongy as beach sand. I'd been in the car too long without a lot of oxygen except for what seeped through the holes in the floor, probably tinged with carbon monoxide. I held onto the door handle until I was sure of my balance. I hoped Tony would notice my hesitation and take my arm, but he didn't.

We crossed the parking lot, a few feet apart. He said, "I hope you like lobster."

"Sure!" I would have said that no matter what, but in fact I really did. Lobsters meant family happiness, special occasions. My family ate them on our brief trips to Atlantic City, and on visits to our old neighborhood, Sheepshead Bay. My husband believed that lobsters were too expensive and too much work. I added lobster to the list of things that Tony and I had in common.

"Good," Tony said. "I could murder a giant crustacean right about now."

It all seemed so normal, going to a restaurant, out on a date, if this *was* a date, having dinner with a friend, if this *was* dinner with a friend, ordering lobster. A night out. I wondered if the breakfast sausage and berry pie at the Martha Washington was a test to see how I reacted. Then I remembered: People knew Tony there. It had nothing to do with me.

They also knew Tony at the Great White Whale, another desolate Edward Hopper scene, only this one with table service, mysterious glass balls trapped in brightly colored fish nets, plaster swordfish and seahorses crucified to the walls. The lighting was seaweed green, and a squadron of melancholy goldfish patrolled the milky tank. There were no families or single customers. The few couples scattered around the room looked gloomy and silent, like adulterers regretting that they'd begun their affair.

A young woman in a sailor dress (Hi, Tony! Hi there, Melissa!) ushered us to a table by a window, and for a while, we just stared across the bay at the ridiculously beautiful city. I wondered what Tony was thinking. I had promised myself never to become the kind of person who asks, What are you thinking? But I didn't have a clue.

Tony had sung along with Harold Melvin and the Blue Notes. *If you don't know me by now, you will never, never, never know me.* I'd always heard the song as a plea for trust. Now I wondered if the song was boasting or complaining.

I lost track of how long the silence lasted. No one took our orders. I looked around. There wasn't a waiter in sight.

I said, "Not to be a downer, but isn't this near the place where Scottie drags Madeleine Elster out of the water?" I was like that girl in college blithering about her uncle's dachshund, except that when I got nervous, I dragged the conversation around to *Vertigo.*

"That's south of here," said Tony. "Old Fort Point. Under the bridge. What a crazy scene. For a few frames the film turns into *Creature from the Black Lagoon,* complete with the dripping-wet, half-dead girl draped across a pair of strong arms. Nobody talks about how Madeleine wakes up in Scottie's bed without any clothes on. The kinkiest scene ever."

Lots of people talked about it. But I wasn't going to say so. I didn't want to discuss the weirdness of Scottie's passion igniting when Madeleine is unconscious. It seemed unlucky to have our first conversation about sex be about Kim Novak waking up naked, after nearly drowning, with perfect makeup and hair.

There was one waiter working. It took him a while to get to us. He wore a tight peacoat and a military cap embossed with a small white whale that he somehow made chic and ironic.

Tony ordered two medium lobsters, two fries, coleslaw, two beers, extra melted butter. He raised his eyebrows at me. I nodded. I wondered if our silent agreement made the waiter think we were a couple. I was embarrassed because I wanted him to think so. If that was how we looked to a stranger, maybe it was true. I wanted it, and I didn't. I didn't want to be part of a couple; I didn't want to be in a "relationship." Maybe I just wanted to be the outlaw sidekick of a famous antiwar hero, the temporary girlfriend of the whistleblower who leaked the Pentagon Papers.

I didn't like beer, which seemed way too cold for the chilly night, but the dark ale brought back a happy childhood memory. I'd gone to New Orleans one summer with my family. It was humid and hot. Everyone was cranky. We stepped into a cool, sweet-smelling, old-fashioned tavern. My brother and I drank 7 Up, and my parents, who weren't big drinkers, had two large beers apiece and were unusually cheerful and patient with us for the rest of that hot afternoon.

The beer at the Great White Whale was exactly what I wanted. We sipped our beers and waited for our lobsters to die.

Tony said, "I saw one of my favorite movies last week. *Kwaidan*. They were showing it in Berkeley. Four Japanese ghost stories that Lafcadio Hearn translated into English and the filmmakers translated back into Japanese. There's one segment about a boy who gets kidnapped by a ghost clan because he sings a beautiful epic poem about the naval battle that wiped out their entire dynasty. They perform it like a Noh play while the boy chants—"

"I saw that film!" I said. "It's the best."

It seemed like another sign. I'd written a short story inspired by the tales in *Kwaidan*. I'd sold it to a magazine, for what had seemed like a lot of money. How could it not mean something that, of all the movies that had ever been made, Tony was a fan of an obscure film that was so important to me?

Kwaidan had precipitated yet another disagreement with my husband, who said the film was shallow and exploitative. I asked how ghost stories could be exploitative or if he was just saying that to annoy me. It was irritating, but also painful, that someone would argue a position just to make me run chemicals that were probably bad for my health.

Tony said, "Lobsters always remind me of the dinner scene in *Tom Jones*. You know the one?"

Of course I knew the brilliant, dirty, hilarious scene from Tony Richardson's 1963 film. For seven minutes Tom (Albert Finney) and Mrs. Waters (Joyce Redman) turn a gluttonous British dinner into juicy elaborate sex. It begins with Tom sucking the tongue of sweet pink meat out of the lobster claw. Mrs. Waters fellates a chicken leg, and it's on. They're having a fabulous time. They think it's a riot.

That was never going to be Tony and me. But the mood between us was warmer than it had been the previous night. Gradual progress, the I Ching would say. Perseverance furthers.

Maybe it was the beer. It was beginning to seem more likely that we would wind up at Tony's apartment. I wanted to sleep with Tony, not out of desire so much as curiosity. I wondered what intimacy with this odd, complicated person would be like.

I used to think that you could tell how a man would be as a lover by how he acted around food—beware the picky and puritanical, seek out the easygoing omnivores—but I didn't know what to make of Tony's love for breakfast sausage, blueberry pie, and lobster. Anyway, you could never predict what sex with someone new would be like. There were always surprises. That was part of what made it exciting.

Tony and I looked at each other and laughed for no reason, the giddy untethered laughter that can mean: Something's going on. Then the waiter returned and tied plastic bibs around our necks, extinguishing whatever dim spark had flickered, turning us back from laughing, mildly aroused adults into hungry obedient babies.

Certain foods are harder to eat around people you don't know well. Crustaceans top the list. You need to be comfortable enough to not worry about spurting green brain matter onto someone's plate. What made it easier was that I might as well have been alone with my food. Tony hunched over his plate, surgically dissecting his lobster like a lab experiment he was being graded on. Meticulous and focused, he dipped the pink meat in butter and closed his eyes when he ate. He was in heaven: a heaven for one. This was not the dinner from *Tom Jones*.

In fact I was grateful. The lobster was delicious, and I could enjoy it in private.

We both ordered coffee. It was no better than the coffee at the Martha Washington, but we drank it down. Butter shone on our lips. We felt warm and full of food. The check came. Tony paid. It was 1974. The rules had changed so that I should have offered to pick up the check, or at least split it, but I didn't.

We got back into the car, and he drove around and around the back roads and through the villages, malls, and parking lots of Marin County.

Pulling onto Highway 101, he said, "What's your favorite book?"

I couldn't think of a single book I'd ever read.

Great Expectations popped into my head. Was it my favorite? I didn't have a favorite.

"Good choice," he said. "I was afraid it was going to be something by Hermann Hesse."

I said, "Seriously? Who do you think I am?"

"Sorry." He laughed. "Henry said you read tarot cards. What do I know? That's what I'm trying to find out. I mean, I'm trying to figure out who you are. Guess *my* favorite book."

I wished he'd spent a few more moments on the subject of who I was or what I liked to read.

I said, "Give me a clue."

"British reporter in Vietnam."

I felt like a *Jeopardy!* contestant. "What is *The Quiet American?*"

"Bingo," Tony said.

As we drove onto the Golden Gate, the lights on the bridge struck stars off his glasses. When he turned to look at me, his eyes glittered, unnaturally bright. Reflexively, I tilted my chin toward the road. We were returning from the relative calm of the coast to the jittery buzz of the city.

Tony said, "*The Quiet American* was the first book I wished I'd written. The first one that made me think that the writer had gotten in my head. I thought it was about *me*. Nothing like that ever happened to me when I was reading as a kid. It probably happened to you all the time. You were probably a big reader. I can see you curled up with a book, in your little schoolgirl uniform."

Little schoolgirl uniform. The phrase creeped me out. Maybe it was the *little*. You didn't write this whole book all by yourself, did you?

I said, "I never wore a uniform. My parents wouldn't let me join the Brownies. The brown shirts made them nervous."

"They were right. Put a uniform on somebody—even a little

girl—and they turn into different people. That was another reason that guys like me had to stay out of the army. Though I guess you could say that I wore a uniform. The short-sleeved drip-dry pocket-protector look was a uniform, the mid-level RAND employee's out-in-the-field uniform, and I wore it proudly."

A lone tear fell and wobbled along the side of his nose. I had to stop from reaching out to touch it.

"Everyone in Saigon was reading *The Quiet American*. There were always extra copies floating around the RAND villa, left behind. Dan wouldn't read it. He said he didn't have time for fiction. But I knew—I still know—whole paragraphs by heart."

Tony pulled to the side of the road, parked the car, sat back, and closed his eyes and was silent until I said, "Like what?"

"'The gold of the rice-fields under a flat late sun: the fishers' fragile cranes hovering over the fields like mosquitoes: the cups of tea on an old abbot's platform, with his bed and his commercial calendars, his buckets and broken cups and the junk of a lifetime washed up around his chair: the mollusc hats of the girls repairing the road where a mine had burst: the gold and the young green and the bright dresses of the south, and in the north the deep browns and the black clothes and the circle of enemy mountains and the drone of planes.'"

He took a deep breath. I applauded.

"Thank you, thank you, thank you," he said. "The weird thing was, in Vietnam I felt like I was both characters, the jaded British reporter *and* the naive idealistic American who steals the Brit's Vietnamese girlfriend. The British guy was living my life, his Saigon was my city. I had such a sweet time there until it all turned to shit. I was just another colonizer thinking I was going to end colonialism, but at least I was trying. I inherited a great apartment above a French restaurant where they made the world's best steak tartare. A hip downscale colonial dream.

"The robots at RAND had zero curiosity. They warned me, Don't eat anything unless you can watch it boil or you see the steam, or you'll get sick as a dog, which by the way they eat, in secret restaurants. If you want to order dog meat, ask for 'traditional food.'

"That's how they talked, our men in Saigon. Racist pieces of shit. Five, six, maybe seven different guys told me the same bullshit urban legend about going to a formal dinner and being served monkey brains out of the skull of a living monkey."

At the end of the bridge, he turned and headed for the Presidio.

"The street food was the best. The pho. You could smell the broth from down the block. That's how you knew where to go. There were a few RAND guys and journalists who really loved the city. We'd trade tips about where to get the best green papaya salad. It got to be a kind of competition, who knew the funkiest place with the fewest tables in the filthiest alley. Mostly the RAND guys ate at the commissary, and *they* were sick all the time. No wonder. If I was a local working in the kitchen at RAND, I'd spit in the food."

I wondered when his diet had devolved into sausage, pie, lobster, and beer, if the link between food and pleasure had been severed during his hunger strike in jail. The problem was not that he didn't enjoy his food. The problem was the food.

"In the novel the British guy tells the American that they're at war with people who aren't interested in fighting. He says, 'They want enough rice. They don't want to be shot at. They want one day to be the same as another. They don't want our white skins around telling them what they want.'

"So here was Greene, in 1956, saying what took me months in Vietnam to figure out. Twenty years later! And the war he was describing was still a French fight. We weren't officially there, though we were already figuring out how to monetize it. It's not a perfect book. The Vietnamese woman is some skimpy silk underwear and a beautiful body that the men pass around while her sister tries to marry her off to any Westerner who can fog a mirror. Greene says *imperialism, colonialism*. He says it straight out, but he's never preaching, just telling the truth."

I was impressed that Tony had memorized so much Graham Greene. In high school we'd been made to memorize the 23rd Psalm and the poems of Robert Frost. I'd had to memorize plenty of information and facts for history and science classes. But except for the first sentence of *One Hundred Years of Solitude*, I had never memorized anything purely out of admiration.

Tony said, "He got it right, what it was like waiting for something bad to happen, for something to blow up. The first place they agreed to let me interview captives and defectors was way out in the field. My translators and I went to the town where the prison was. There was no one around. No prison. No nothing. It was a ghost town. Eerie. There was one dark café with a single table. We went inside and had coffee while we tried to figure out what to do.

"When we go back outside, someone has left a piaster bill— North Vietnamese currency—on the front seat of our car. A little sign. A little warning. Welcome to town from the National Liberation Front. We're watching you. Just so you know. We have no reason to kill you. Yet."

Tony drove on a few blocks, then swerved and stopped again, this time facing a park. Before his headlights went out, they illuminated a row of tightly pruned trees like prickly black lollipops.

"A ten-dong bill with a portrait of handsome young Ho Chi Minh."

"What did you do?"

Tony shrugged. "We found the prison. Someone showed us the way. We did the interviews. We got through it. We went back to Saigon and got crazy drunk."

"Whom did you interview? Do you remember?"

He shook his head. If I didn't ask again, maybe he'd stop crying.

He said, "The Greene book reminds me what it was like to be there. Otherwise it's all a dream. What happened to all that time? That place? Where did it go? There's this one passage—the journalist looks down and sees he's got a paunch. I didn't have one then, but I'm getting one now. I'm turning into the sad old Brit."

"Wrong accent," I said.

Tony smiled. "I've grown into my Southern accent. Maybe it's even got a bit stronger. I don't know why that would be. Certain people seem to like it."

By *certain people*, I suspected, Tony meant *women*.

At that time, that was the case for me, and I wondered what Henry and Grace had told Tony.

The previous year, I'd had a boyfriend, Emmet, who was born in the South. I liked to think that I missed his accent more than anything else, but I knew that was one of those glib things I thought to protect myself from the complicated truth.

Tony said, "If guys aren't from the South, they think the accent means you're stupid. People liked me fine at Princeton. They thought I was funny. Especially the foreign students. Some of my fellow Americans didn't think I was all that bright. My professors took personal pride in lifting up the hillbilly genius whiz kid. Teaching me to eat something besides grits and pork rinds gave them a warm, fuzzy feeling.

"Anyway, Princeton was like Disneyland compared to later, when I was at RAND, especially at the end. Doors slammed shut when I walked by. It got kind of Pavlovian. I'd say good morning and everyone stood and walked out of the room."

"Sounds sort of like graduate school." What did I even mean? My fellow students hadn't *tried* to make me uncomfortable; they just did. And how could I compare my sad little bout of academic alienation with Tony's having been frozen out by war profiteers disguised as statistical analysts? Asking a nun to translate dirty stories from Middle English was not the same as factoring the bulk price of Agent Orange into the projected budget of the defoliation campaign.

I saw Tony almost every night. We still hadn't had sex. I'd never even been to his apartment. It was puzzling. I'd slept with men with whom I'd spent a fraction of that time and who interested me far less. I reminded myself to be patient and to have no expectations.

Things between us were unclear. We were more than friends, but what were we? Tony hadn't touched me except when he'd helped me put on my jacket. I didn't think he was gay. I didn't know what to think. It was fine with me, at least for a while, if everything stayed the way it was. At that time, people often acted, or tried to act, as if sex meant nothing, as if it were just another form of recreation. But just as often it changed everything in unpredictable ways.

Sometimes, when Tony picked me up in his car, he didn't say hello or bother with small talk. It was as if he was pausing from a heated discussion he'd been having with himself.

He said, "Do I seem forgettable to you? Do you think you would remember me if you met me a second time?"

"Yes," I said. "I'd remember." For once, I didn't hesitate.

"Dan didn't remember meeting me in Saigon. It wasn't until we had offices across the hall at RAND that we became friends. We had lots to talk about—whisper, really—because if anyone heard us . . ." He slashed a finger across his throat and laughed.

"Those first conversations . . . You can't imagine how it felt, finally being able to say what we'd kept inside for so long. The nightmares, the horrors, plus all the good stuff—how Saigon felt on a sultry night, the sweetness of the people—all that only made the horrors worse."

It was absurd to feel jealous of Ellsberg for hearing what Tony couldn't tell anyone else, for hearing it for the first time. I knew that it was ridiculous. But I couldn't help it.

"Dan was scared of me at first. *Imperialism. Criminal aggression. Capitalism. Genocide. Military-industrial complex.* The words I used made his blood run cold. So I said them as often as I could. You know what that's like. Feeling compelled to say the one thing you're not supposed to say . . ."

I did know. During a seminar that managed to make Coleridge boring, I told the class that I'd smoked a lot of opium and never felt anything like what inspired "Kubla Khan." I invented an opium-addict friend with Hong Kong connections. I talked about how sick I'd gotten in disgusting detail. The silence got heavier. Our untenured assistant professor stared at me with what might have been curiosity or pity, but which I read as hatred.

"Dan looked for me at RAND," Tony said. "He sought me out. He was halfway out the door to being a radical, but he stopped in the doorway. He didn't want to find himself on the outside, like me, because by then, our bosses had ID'd me as a serious pain in their corporate ass. I'd been fired for telling the truth about torture, the pacification program, all the wicked shit they were doing. They gave me a six-month grace period to . . . I don't know . . . clean out my desk. Plan the festive retirement party. Hire the chorus girl to jump out of the cake.

"That was their big mistake. If they hadn't let me stick around, Dan and I would never have become friends.

"They wanted me to say I was leaving because of health issues, but I wouldn't say that. So they claimed they were letting me go for budgetary reasons. That was bullshit too. My salary was peanuts compared to what the top-tier guys were making. Dan was the only one who stuck up for me. I thought that's who he was. Mr. Stand-Up. Mr. Got Your Back. Mr. With You All the Way.

"Our friendship took a while to unravel, but I know, pretty much to the minute, when it snapped. At a formal dinner in Chicago. Dan was speaking. He'd asked me to say a few words. I'd just gotten out of jail. I was still wearing the T-shirt and corduroys I'd worn in prison. I was the only non-penguin in the room. Once I got to the microphone, I really wanted to talk. Maybe because I'd been in solitary, maybe I'd gotten high on the ride over, maybe I'd had too much time to think. I started talking, and I couldn't stop. I forgot who my audience was. I forgot that Dan was waiting for me to shut the fuck up. I started speaking from the heart."

"Always a mistake," I said.

"*Big* mistake. I don't know what I said. Later someone told me that I'd talked till past midnight. People were getting up to go home. Apparently I ranted about the Attica prison uprising, about the hunger strike I was planning in solidarity with America's convict class, about how fashionable it was to oppose the war. I *really* should not have said *that*. I talked about how hard it was to do anything about poverty, injustice, mass incarceration, I talked about capitalism and genocide. Until I was gently, or not so gently, ushered offstage. As they perp-walked me out of the room, I heard Dan tell what was left of the crowd, 'When you decide to change the world, I hope you have a friend like this very hungry and very brave man.'"

"He was on your side," I said. "He was trying to help—"

"*A friend like this*," Tony repeated, and was silent for a long time. "Hilarious. *This very hungry and brave man.* Hungry? I'd been en route from prison around the time they'd been serving the rubber chicken at the fundraising dinner. Is *that* what he meant?"

"Tony, the window wipers," I said. "It's really raining."

"Right," said Tony. "Got it. Click. You know what Dan's favorite film was?"

I couldn't guess. Godard, I thought. "*Breathless?*"

"*Butch Cassidy and the Sundance Kid.* He must have watched it a dozen times. I think that's who he thought we were: two handsome movie-star outlaw buddies fighting a corrupt, degraded system."

It was sweet, in a nerdy way, Daniel Ellsberg imagining himself and Tony as Paul Newman and Robert Redford. It wasn't so unlike my obsession with *Bonnie and Clyde.* Another chaste and doomed outlaw romance. It wasn't completely different, though obviously it wasn't the same.

"Dan and I felt responsible. We should have spoken up earlier. We'd been on the wrong side. The *really* wrong side. The deaths, the bombing, the napalm, the orphaned kids, the anguished old people. We weren't just passive onlookers. We'd contributed to the war—first with our expertise, then with our silence. That's why we had to leak the papers to the press."

"You were right," I said.

"Fuckin' A, we were right. I keep telling myself I've paid my dues. Made amends. I no longer have blood on my hands. But denying that you have blood on your hands means that you have blood on your hands. I'm your policy-wonk radical Lady Macbeth. I was lonely until I met Dan. And we trusted each other. We did. We talked each other into committing a federal crime.

"When reporters asked whose idea it was, I'd say, Who cares? I still don't care. Or maybe I do, a little. Probably I wouldn't care at all if I'd gotten any credit. If I hadn't sat in my apartment and watched, on TV, Dan getting a standing ovation on the fucking Dick Cavett show.

"That benefit dinner in Chicago, when they wanted to shut me up, I was waiting for Dan to finish, and I noticed a card, a place card on the table right where I was sitting. Know what it said?"

It wasn't really a question, but I shook my head no, if only to remind him that I was there.

"It said, 'Friend of Daniel Ellsberg.' Friend of Daniel Ellsberg! They knew goddamn well that I was Anthony Russo. Friend of Daniel Ellsberg? They were fucking with me. They? I always thought it was Pat. Pat Ellsberg. I thought she personally wrote out that card to put me in my place, so to speak, to get back at me just because my name was on the indictment, because I was named first—"

The faster he talked, the faster he drove. The road was slick with rain.

I said, "I don't know, Tony. I can't imagine Pat Ellsberg writing out place cards for that dinner."

"Not for the whole room. Just our table. Ten seats. She could have done it. But why am I telling you this? It's not supposed to matter. It doesn't matter. We were trying to stop a war. I'd just gotten out of prison. Who cares about a place card?"

"You're right," I said. "It doesn't—"

"But then when they were *escorting* me away, and Dan said, 'I hope you have a friend like this,' et cetera. *Friend of Daniel Ells-*

berg. That's what the card said. It was weird. I had to wonder if Dan and Pat were working something out, and I got caught in the crossfire. Right?"

"I don't know," I said.

"Why am I asking you? If the papers had shortened the war by even one day, I wouldn't have given a shit. But by the time we went on trial, the bombing of Laos was off the charts, another open secret. And then, by some bizarre twist of fate, the plumbers who got caught burglarizing Dan's shrink got Nixon's ass kicked out of the Oval Office. Don't you writers say, You can't make this shit up?"

You writers. It still surprised me that someone would include me in that group. It made me unreasonably happy.

"That's what we say," I said, though I had never said that in my life.

I thought I understood what might have happened at that dinner. It was either the start or the end of a marketing calculation: Let's say you had to choose between two men—two friends who carried out the copying and release of the Pentagon Papers. One was going to be interviewed on TV, getting peace prizes, being the keynote speaker at conferences and galas. The other was unkempt and outspoken and upset everyone when he talked like the radical left. You'd pick the first one, the handsome one, the more moderate one, the less extreme one, the guy less likely to make people nervous, the guy with the good haircut. That one was Daniel Ellsberg.

Only one of the two would go to jail. That one was Tony Russo.

Tony's *New York Times* obituary, dated August 8, 2008, describes him as "a shaggy-haired, countercultural, unemployed policy wonk when he teamed up with Daniel Ellsberg, a more buttoned-down antiwar figure, to leak the voluminous, top secret government history of the Vietnam War called the Pentagon Papers."

In fact, Tony had the one thing that Ellsberg didn't have, which was charm. *Charm* isn't a word you'd associate with Ellsberg. *Intensity*, sure. *Passion*, sure. But *charm?* Tony had charm to spare. It comes through in his essays and in the film clip of him talking about the time when he thought he was going to jail. But charm is harder to sell than beauty, and there are many people for whom words like *genocide* and *colonialism* instantly vaporize the pleasant effects of charm.

Once, it had been fine to use certain words, and afterward it wasn't. It had been cool to want to change the world, but it began to seem embarrassing. Once, you could let your hair grow long and unkempt, but by 1974, you were supposed to clean up. You were expected to rethink, and even apologize for, the impossible things you'd wanted. If you'd gone to sleep envisioning a world in which money no longer mattered, you woke up understanding that it was a better idea to earn as much as you could.

Tony didn't often repeat himself, but there was one story, about his former boss, that he kept returning to:

"Sometimes Dr. Strangelove would take us out to sightsee the war, except that he called it *a field study* or some such bullshit. He'd take us to a beach resort, and we'd sit in deck chairs sipping umbrella drinks and watching bombs explode across the bay, like fireworks except that the explosions were on the ground. It was like watching a war movie at a drive-in, except that it was real. Blobs of fire were erupting all over. And they were killing people. He'd raise his glass with its little tiny umbrella and toast the bombing. Toast the war. With his fucking mai tais. He wanted more bombs. More war. More scorched earth. Increased air power. He wanted to tell the military what they wanted to hear. He wanted to please the air force, which provided a large part of RAND's funding. He sent us out to collect data that would prove that he was right. And no one tried to stop him.

"We had drinks with the guy. We gave him what he wanted, shut up and let it happen because it meant that we were still on the payroll and theoretically able to keep him from going more rogue, getting away with more murder, until we couldn't stand it, and we said something, or did something, and we got fired and became pariahs. I say *we*, but I mean *me*. I was the one who put my ass on the line. It was like eighth grade. You all agree to play some joke on the teacher, and your buddies bail without telling you, and you're the only one who goes ahead with the joke. And the joke's on you."

I didn't say that I'd heard the story before. I let him tell it. I listened. We were parked near the de Young Museum. A man and a dog walked in front of us across the lawn. Lit by the moon, the ghost man and his ghost dog appeared and dissolved into the mist. Like a special effect in a horror film. The Incredible Vanishing Dog Walker.

"Did you see that? Psychedelic," Tony said. "Another thing about *The Quiet American* is that our narrator is deep into opium. No judgment, it's Vietnam. Everyone smokes. His girlfriend makes up pipes for him. It's like his after-work martini. After three pipes he's worry-free, but he can function. I tried opium once at a friend's house. I vomited and fell asleep and didn't shit for a week. Not my drug of choice. Have you tried it?"

"Once. A friend had a little chunk and we smoked it in a foil pipe. I was fine—just a little sleepy—until my friend's room-mate came home with a carton of peppermint-stick ice cream and I took one look at it and threw up for the rest of the night."

"What about LSD? Dan and I used to say that RAND was in the LSD business. Lies, Secrecy, and Deceit."

Tony didn't seem remotely judgmental, but still I didn't want him to see me as someone who had taken a lot of acid. I didn't tell many people that I had. I feared that strangers would as-sume it meant that I wasn't a serious person. But something about Tony made me want to be honest.

I said, "I took it whenever I could. I loved how everything got brighter and more interesting. I liked how the trees would begin to sing that funny high-pitched song. I was nervous the first few times, but I never hallucinated. When everyone was tripping their brains out, I was the person who could talk on the phone when someone's mom called."

In fact I had hallucinated once. But that was a long and com-plicated story, and I didn't want to tell it. It was about Emmet, whom I didn't want to think about right then.

"And now? Do you still take LSD?"

"Every so often I take it with some friends who go camping on the beach in Mendocino. But I feel like it's gotten . . . familiar. I still enjoy it, but I feel as if the drug has less to give me, that maybe hearing the trees sing isn't worth being knocked out for the next three days."

"And you never had a bad time?"

I shook my head. Not bad, strictly speaking. Just strange.

A year before, I'd imagined that I was in love. I'd met Emmet in San Francisco. Another friend of Henry and Grace's, he was born in Tennessee but grew up in Alaska, near the Arctic Circle, where his father built radio satellites to track Russian missiles flying over the Bering Strait. He had dropped out of college, but he'd read more than most of the graduate students I'd known.

He'd been to Afghanistan. He'd lived for a while in Kabul, where he made his living exporting hashish in tiny pieces knotted into area rugs decorated with John F. Kennedy's portrait. He'd recently come back from Asia and was staying on Henry and Grace's living room couch. One night, when we were alone, sitting on opposite sides of the room, he patted the couch beside him and said, "Come over here, okay?" After that we both lived in my room.

Every day Emmet and I walked across the city, from the Sunset to North Beach and back, to the Presidio and back, to the Embarcadero and back. He had a flawless sense of direction that, he said, came from driving a dogsled across the frozen tundra. He told a lot of stories that no one could check up on. He claimed to have survived a tornado that lifted the family car and dropped it a few blocks away. He said that his life's ambition was to be a storm chaser, one of those people who head into the eye of a hurricane and report on it for the evening news.

Once, we spent two weeks in the backyard cabin of some friends of his, outside Tucson. We walked out into the desert for hours, through the saguaro cactus forests and up and down arroyos, and we never once got lost. I have a good memory for landmarks, so I can find my way if I've been somewhere before, but I have no inner compass, not like Emmet had. I was always astonished when we got back to where we'd started.

That fall, I sold two stories to a magazine for $600 apiece. The first story was called "Youthful Folly." The title came from a hexagram in the I Ching. It was another tale within a tale, this one set in Japan. That was the one I wrote after seeing *Kwaidan*, the film made from the Lafcadio Hearn ghost stories. The second story the magazine bought was called "Bondage." The narrator was the widow of Harry Houdini, though she isn't called that. I no longer have a copy, but I remember that the first line went something like "Whenever I said that I was the great magician's wife, people always thought of the dirty things first."

Twelve hundred dollars was more than I'd gotten for my novel. Emmet and I decided to take the money and go to Mexico until the money ran out.

The magazine editor said that "Youthful Folly" had to be cut by several thousand words. I asked her to please go ahead and cut it; I was going to Mexico. She had reservations about publishing a story called "Bondage" in a general-interest woman's magazine. I asked her to please suggest another title.

Emmet and I took the train, a sleeper car, from Nogales to Mexico City, a ride so rocky that we had to hold each other tightly to keep from rolling off the bunk bed. In the capital we found a cheap hotel with rooms that surrounded a central atrium built around a giant palm tree. It was on Isabel la Católica, and though I knew that Queen Isabella had expelled the Jews from Spain and sent Columbus to plunder the so-called New World, I thought it was the loveliest street name I'd ever heard. I remember taking a nap with my head on Emmet's lap, on one of the massive stone benches in the courtyard of the National Anthropological Museum, and being woken by a guard telling us, politely and almost regretfully, that I couldn't sleep there.

We traveled east to the Yucatan, on a train we shared with a small flock of chickens that the passengers conspired to hide from the conductor.

We were headed for the Mayan temple at Palenque. According to Emmet, they'd found, deep inside the pyramid, a stone carving of a god that looked so much like an extraterrestrial piloting a spaceship that even conservative academics were beginning to theorize that the Mayans had been visited and possibly kidnapped by aliens. Emmet had a flat affect and a drawl that slowed down even more when he talked about extraterrestrials, astronomy, and stormy weather. He stated most things as if they were facts about which he had no opinion.

Emmet had never been to Palenque, but he walked through the town as if he had always lived there, and led us straight to a pretty hotel with dark cool rooms around a courtyard landscaped with lush tropical plants.

A narrow band of light filtered into our room from an open space between the wall and the roof. I heard something scurry across the wall.

"Geckos," said Emmet. "Harmless. Don't worry. They're smarter than we are. And they don't want to come near us."

The smell—cleaning soap, damp plaster, darkness—was sweet. Being there felt like hiding out: Bonnie and Clyde holed up in Palenque.

In the fields outside Palenque, some hippies from Quebec, camping in a pasture, were cooking eggs with the psilocybin mushrooms they'd harvested from the edges of cow patties. They offered us wedges of omelet, on a paper napkin, to Emmet and me. How could we say no? The mushroom omelet was delicious, the dosage hard to quantify. *Bon appétit!* Everyone laughed. The Quebecois were extremely high and happy to be so far from the Canadian winter.

We should have had one bite and saved the rest for later, but that would have seemed rude.

Emmet and I had the good sense to hitch a ride in a pickup

truck with some friendly farmers and get back to our hotel room just as the mushrooms were coming on.

We lay in bed, on our backs, fully dressed, holding hands. I was wondering how to say, in my bad Spanish, that my boyfriend and I had overdosed on *hongos*. After I stopped having pointlessly sequential thoughts, after I stopped asking myself questions that turned into bright-colored neon blobs hitting cartoon brick walls, I relaxed. I watched transparent jellyfish float in the dark, morphing into amoebae, half fireworks, half lava lamp. I waited for it to end. That was the only time I hallucinated. But the lights were just entertainment: the floor show. I never forgot the number of our hotel room or where I kept our passports.

There was one low moment when I was washing socks in the bathroom sink. I was weeping about mortality and why true love never lasted. Somehow I made it back to bed. Emmet and I didn't have to talk. It was enough to know that he was there, alive and breathing. I understood that I was being shown what love could be like, but that this wasn't it. The voice of love would be another voice, on other nights, in a different darkness. This was like watching a trailer, a preview of things to come.

There was a knock on the door. A woman said, "Hey. It's Rosalind. Are you there?"

We'd met Rosalind on the train to Palenque. She was a writer. I'd recognized her because she had just published a book of feminist essays about a woman's right to sleep with whoever she wants and not get her ass pinched by strangers. Her book had made enough of a splash to put her photo in newspapers and magazines. The way she looked at us made it obvious that she couldn't understand what another published woman writer was doing with a stoner hillbilly like Emmet.

The mushrooms had erased big chunks of the recent past,

including our telling Rosalind that she could leave her backpack in our room. She wasn't spending the night in Palenque, just checking out the temple.

Emmet let her in. I was too high to get out of bed. I said I wasn't feeling well. But I was sober enough to worry about Rosalind, traveling alone, a pretty young woman with a backpack, in a low-cut T-shirt, boots, and army shorts.

I told Tony, "I felt guilty for forgetting about her, and for finding her sort of annoying, and only then, thanks to the mushrooms, did I understand that Rosalind was the Buddha. I asked her if she wanted to get a room in the hotel, but she was on her way. She had plans."

I stopped. Maybe I'd said too much. I'd sounded like a spoiled hippie brat, taking mushrooms in Mexico while Tony was recovering from arrest, imprisonment, and trial.

"The Buddha," said Tony. "That's rich. What happened to her? The writer?"

I fought a shaming snobbish desire to say, Well, Rosalind isn't *exactly a writer.* Because she was. Rosalind was a writer.

I said, "She's fine, I guess. Someone told me she's working on another book."

When Emmet and I finally came down from the mushrooms, we went back out to the temple and watched the sun set over the ruins. He had a raw, beautiful voice, and he sang a Southern hymn about fire raining down from heaven and blood filling the sea and being carried home by Jesus.

Our love affair ran out before the money from the magazine did. It had been fun to travel with Emmet, to shower together in the whitewashed bathrooms of cheap Mexican hotels. But neither he nor I could imagine a future together on either coast, or anywhere except on the road, and we couldn't travel forever.

I wept when Emmet and I left Mérida in different directions.

He was taking the train back to LA, and I was flying to New York via Miami.

I called my parents from a phone booth in the Miami airport to tell them that I had left Mexico and was coming home to Manhattan. They took turns reading me the rave review of my novel that had appeared that day in the *New York Times.*

I decided, superstitiously, that the praise was my reward for hardly thinking about my novel or its reception the whole time I'd been in Mexico. The good review had nothing to do with the book. It was about my having worked some kind of magic. I'd read that the alchemists believed that you could make gold if you performed the entire chemical process without once thinking of the word *hippopotamus.*

I was shocked, even more than I'd been when Harry said he wanted to publish my novel. I'd seen the galley proofs and the finished copy, but until then I hadn't believed that any of it was real. It had seemed impossible that my book would have a life outside my imagination, an independent existence. Apparently at least one person besides my parents, Harry, his thuggish boss, and me believed that I was a writer.

I burst into tears as my parents took turns reading the *Times* critic's description of a book that sounded so much better than the one I wrote. On the plane from Mérida, I'd cried about leaving Emmet, so maybe I'd primed the pump, and my tears flowed more readily than they otherwise would have. I continued to cry as the phone booth got hotter and steamier and I noticed a line of travelers pantomiming their need to make calls. My father read me the last sentence. I told my parents that I loved them and apologized to the people waiting and ran to catch my plane.

"Youthful Folly" ran in the magazine, several thousand

words shorter. I never missed one word that was cut. After much back-and-forth, "Bondage" appeared in the same magazine under the title "Bondage."

The memory of hearing my parents read me the review was vivid and distracting. Just thinking about it felt like getting good news on a difficult day.

It took me a beat to focus on what Tony was saying:

"I don't know how much Henry and Grace told you," he said, "but for a while, I had some trouble getting my head straight after the jail and the trial plus after . . . some . . . *misunderstandings* with Dan. First I thought he wasn't going to go through with releasing the papers. That was around the time he got married. Pat, his wife, never liked me. She did everything to come between us. I was too shaggy, too unpredictable, too unfashionable, too weird. And *way* too radical. Insufficiently coiffed. She convinced Dan that he was the fairy-tale prince and I was the troll who lived under the bridge.

"I can't blame her for what Dan did. No one makes him do anything he doesn't want to do. No one except me. He's way crazier than I am, but everyone thinks he's the reasonable one, the middle-of-the-road guy, and I'm the commie radical conspiring to bomb your house and have sex on acid with your underage daughter. It weighed on me, plus the daily harassment, the cops cruising past my house, looking for any excuse to send me back to jail.

"A friend suggested I take a break, spend a weekend at Esalen. It didn't sound like my kind of place, an upscale tree-hugger summer camp in the middle of nowhere. But my rich friend offered to pay for my stay, and the place was supposed to be beautiful. What did I have to lose?

154 • FRANCINE PROSE

"Everyone was friendly, though, to be honest, I'd gotten used to people recognizing me, and I was surprised when no one did."

"*I* knew who you were," I said.

"I *know* you did," said Tony. "The Esalen people weren't 'into politics,' which was irritating. But hey, it was only a weekend. What could go wrong?"

I'd never thought of Tony as someone who wanted to be recognized, who wanted attention and praise for what he'd done. If I'd had to guess, I would have said that he was 85 percent pure idealism, 15 percent egoism. But doesn't everyone harbor a secret vanity that sticks to us, even if we try to shake it off or hide it?

"They took the holistic purification thing very seriously, but when it got late, the partygoers separated out from the I-need-my-eight-hours-of-beauty-sleep crowd, and naturally I went with the party.

"They knew where the hot springs were. Someone had acid. Everyone was naked. I don't know what I expected. I expected it to be fun. I expected—okay, let's be honest here—I expected, I *hoped*, that if things worked out, maybe I'd have sex with one of the women. People said that's what happened there. I'd heard that *hot springs* was Esalen code-speak for *orgy.*"

If Tony and I had been having sex, that part of the story wouldn't have meant anything. A detail, a setup for something or nothing. It would have gone right by me. But we weren't having sex, so I wondered: Is this his way of saying that he wanted—*wants*—sex with other women, but not with me?

"I guess that I was imagining your basic naked-hot-springs good time. Instead of which, things got very dark. Very fast. The acid hit, and boom. I hallucinated blood, bombs, dead children, a nonstop film loop repeating in my head. Every nightmare I saw in Vietnam. All the really grisly shit. I thought I'd put the worst of it out of my mind until the drug said, Surprise, Tony! We're still here!"

Tony rubbed his eyes with his wrist.

"They said I screamed for an hour. I nuked the party right out of existence. The next morning the head guru called me into his super-luxe handmade-cabin office and asked me to leave Esalen. He suggested I seek help. He gave me a list of therapists in the greater Los Angeles area. I wanted to ask, What's the head honcho of Esalen doing with a list of LA therapists? Are you guys generating referrals? Are you all in this together? The situation was doing nothing for my paranoia."

"And did you?"

"Did I what?"

"Leave."

"Gladly. I tried to get my friend a refund, but that wasn't going to happen."

"*Did* you contact one of the therapists?" I couldn't believe I'd asked something so personal. I hardly breathed till he said, "Hell, no. But that was the last time I took LSD. I got into DMT for a while. It made everything really interesting, but also quick and violent, and when you came down, *nothing* was interesting. In fact everything was insanely dull and depressing."

I wished I weren't thinking about taking psilocybin in Mexico. I wished I weren't feeling sorry for myself for not being somewhere else. I wished I weren't longing to be watching the sunset from the steps of a Mayan temple instead of parked beside a patch of weeds, hearing about Tony's freak-out in the Esalen hot springs. I wished I weren't so snobbish that I thought Esalen was dorky. I wished I weren't so shallow that I missed a man who'd imported hash in JFK rugs when I was sitting beside an antiwar hero who had leaked the Pentagon Papers and gone to jail in defense of our democracy. I wished it had nothing to do with sex.

I said, "Do you think you can drive me home? I need to get up in the morning." It was true, sort of. I didn't like lying to Tony. It wasn't a lie. I had to wake up in the morning, even if no one cared what time I awoke or whether I got out of bed.

"Fine. As long as we can do this again tomorrow night," he said.

"Sure," I heard myself say. "Just tell me when."

The next day Tony called me at Henry and Grace's to say that something had come up. He needed to reschedule. Could we meet the following night?

I was way too disappointed. That should have been a warning.

But sure. It was fine. I'd see him tomorrow.

That evening, I visited my friend Moira, who lived in the Reno, the former boxers' hotel in the Mission. With its redwood beams and old-wood paneling, her loft had the feel of a barn or an eccentric artist's frontier cabin somewhere in the Wild West, like the interior sets in *McCabe and Mrs. Miller*.

Moira ran a film distribution company and made short films. One of her films was an anthology of brief interviews with redheads; Moira herself had a startling nimbus of curly red hair. In another of her films, "Folly," less than a minute long, a woman in a Victorian costume walks along the beach, trying to sweep the waves back into the ocean with a broom. Moira was separated from her filmmaker husband, Nick. Around dinnertime, their little son, Amos, was usually splashing around, bathing in Moira's kitchen sink.

Once, Amos took me and Henry on a guided tour of the

Reno, of the abandoned upper floors where no one lived, and which were probably unsafe. As a very small child, Amos had learned how to navigate the blocked and broken corridors. He knew every iffy floorboard. Backlit by the strobe-like flashes from the air shafts, he looked like a magical boy. He led us to his private hideout, a room he had fixed up to look like those elaborate Halloween displays people set up on their front porches, gauzy webs and a woolly spider over a mattress on the floor.

"I decorated it myself," Amos said.

"Very cool," said Henry.

I said, "Does your mom know about this?"

"She's been here," said Amos. "She likes it."

Moira had taught me how to read tarot. She'd been doing it for years. On my own I'd learned what I could about the deck, the meaning of the cards and the ceremony of reading them.

Now she laid out the cards on her flour-streaked, farm-oak kitchen table.

Lots of swords turned up. The Hanged Man. The Tower.

Near the end of *Gravity's Rainbow*, Pynchon provides a detailed tarot reading for his arch villain, Weissmann. The German's significator, the knight of swords ("the rider on a black horse, charging in a gallop neither he nor the horse can control across the heath over the giant grave-mounds") is crossed by the Tower. The designers of the deck, we're told, believed that the Tower represents splendor and victory over an avenging force, but most other interpretations are neither so violent nor so triumphant. If the Tower comes up, you can tell the person you're reading for that it signifies a radical overturning of old habits and outgrown ideas, but few people are going to look at the crumbling, lightning-struck tower and believe you.

Moira said, "You know too much about this for me to bullshit you about the old making way for the new. About bad times coming to an end and promising new beginnings. About overcoming the past to make room for the future. You can see as well as I can that something—you know that it never says *what*, exactly—is going to end badly."

I'd told her a little about Tony, not much: who he was and how I'd met him and how much time we'd spent driving around the city. I wanted her to assure me that the tarot's warning wasn't about him, but I was afraid to ask. She'd only repeat that I knew what the cards meant. I knew as well as she did.

One night, driving Tony's favorite loop, out to the end of the Sunset district and back through Outer Richmond, he said, "Sometime between the day I got subpoenaed and the day I was arrested, I stopped feeling comfortable in my own home, which is not a warm, cozy feeling. Maybe, just maybe, that was because two FBI agents were parked across the street 24/7. Navy Crown Vic, the same cheap blue as their suits. I moved to a safe house. I didn't feel safe there either, but it was marginally better.

"I didn't ask—I didn't want to know—who had stayed there before me. But whoever it was had left behind a book, an art book, images of the devil down through the centuries. There was a Renaissance painting of falling angels, ugly motherfuckers with forked tongues and pointy ears, tumbling from heaven into the flames, their faces contorted, screaming. I remember thinking how ironic for the devils to fall all that way and wind up in Italian suits in the corner offices at RAND in lovely Santa Monica.

"At first RAND had uniformed cops patrolling the lobby, but later the guards wore blazers, so they'd look like guys waiting around to go to lunch at the club. The office isn't far from the Santa Monica freeway, but I'm not sure that qualifies as hell, do you?"

I said, "I don't really know Los Angeles. People talk about the freeways by number, and everyone knows what they mean except me." I'd been to LA twice. When I was thirteen, I'd gone with my parents to visit Disneyland. The second time, not long after I got married, we'd gone out to visit my husband's best friend—the one I slept with in San Francisco—who was spending the summer in Venice Beach. He drove us up to Mono Lake, in the Sierras, where we all took acid. That was the sum total of my knowledge of the city.

"Crazy town," said Tony. "It goes on forever. You'd think that would make it a great place to disappear, except for the police helicopters tracking you from the sky. Maybe we could drive down to LA. Take a road trip. Stay with friends. I could get rearrested. Joking!"

One night, bumping along Webster Street, Tony said, "When I was still in LA, I asked my doctor to try an experiment. He hooked me up to the blood pressure cuff, and when he said 'Saigon,' my pressure shot up. I don't think it's supposed to work like that, but that's what happened."

If Tony's blood pressure was high, maybe it had something to do with the breakfast sausage, the blueberry pie, and lobster. The high-speed driving. I knew that I was underestimating his guilt, his grief, and what he'd been through in Saigon. He would never forgive his bosses. He said he would never get over it without becoming a Buddhist, but he didn't have the patience for long silences, and he could never give up meat.

He said, "I wish I could separate my memories of Saigon from my memories of Dr. Strangelove. He was Russian. His family lost everything in the revolution, so his hatred of communists was very personal and very real. So what if Russian communists were different from the North Vietnamese? Communists were communists, and he wanted them all dead. There weren't enough fighter jets in the world to bomb them out of existence.

"He was our fearless leader. Our Captain Kirk. Strangelove had the perfect accent, a musical rolling baritone, a Continental high-culture delivery. He sounded like a museum director. That's what he should have been except that the art wouldn't spill enough blood to satisfy his vampire thirst.

"Everybody kissed his ass. Every office has one of those guys. The team falls silent when they talk. They alone can be heard in the noisy room. It's the same everywhere. The difference was that our team had green-lighted a lot of murder.

"That's why Dan and I were friends. We could talk about the moment when we first *knew* that our soldiers were committing war crimes, when we first understood that we had blood on our hands."

"When was that?" I said. "The moment it turned."

"That's another story," Tony said. "For another night."

Every battle has its Achilles sulking in his tent. Every war reminds us that some humans react badly when they find themselves surrounded by slaughter and gore, that some of us are terrified by the fact that someone is trying to kill us. Some soldiers don't take to the horror and don't snap back the minute it ends. The changing terms for the psychic damage of war reflect the evolving ideas about its nature and causes: Cowardice is the oldest of these terms, and the penalty for cowardice was death.

Ultimately, the more understanding and less punitive military doctors who treated World War I veterans renamed it. Among the kindest and most sympathetic of the new diagnoses was "muscular exhaustion of the heart." Irritable heart. Shell disorder. Shell explosion paralysis. Disordered action of the heart.

Shell shock became an admissible verdict in military trials—as opposed to, say, desertion, still a capital crime. *Shell shock* was not just a metaphor, but a literal description of the result of huddling in a trench while mortars rained down and shook the earth.

During the war in Vietnam, cases increased enough to merit yet another diagnostic term. In 1972, the *New York Times* reported on the so-called post-Vietnam syndrome. Its symptoms were "growing apathy, cynicism, alienation, depression, mistrust and expectations of betrayal, as well as an inability to concentrate, insomnia, nightmares, restlessness, uprootedness, and impatience with any job or course of study." Not long ago, I watched a documentary about a group of Vietnam veterans who had suffered for decades and who were helped by a kind of psychedelic reset, a parallel experience—this time a positive one, with ayahuasca in the Andes.

It wasn't until the 1980s that the concept of trauma acquired the range of meanings it has now. The diagnostic term *PTSD*, post-traumatic stress disorder, spread retroactively back to the veterans of Vietnam, forward to Iraq and Afghanistan, and to many other kinds of trauma aside from the military.

I don't know what was "wrong" with Tony. I certainly didn't know then. If I had to guess now, I'd say that one of his problems was disappointment. Disappointment on a major scale. The disappointment of thinking that he was going to change the course of history and not changing much of anything except the course of his own career. Disappointment with his friend Dan, disappointment with his country for not thanking him for trying to save lives, disappointment with our democracy for punishing him for attempting to defend the Constitution.

If I think that Tony might have had PTSD, it's partly because I have since met two men who cried exactly the way he did, at precisely the same sort of moments. Both had been to Vietnam, and both told me, with a mixture of embarrassment and pride, that they'd been diagnosed with post-traumatic stress disorder, and that none of the therapies they'd tried— experiments that had been tried *on them*—had helped, even slightly.

One night, over another dinner in Sausalito, Tony said, "What made everything crystal clear was the jury selection for our trial. The voir dire. When I heard what our lawyers weren't allowed to ask prospective jurors, I remembered why I was there, why I was willing to go to jail, why I wouldn't go to jail if we got the jury we wanted because those jurors would know that we'd done the right thing.

"Our lawyers tried to exclude the kind of middle-aged white guy who'd eaten huge amounts of shit in his life and didn't see why Dan and I shouldn't eat some too. Why were *we* rocking the boat? Those are the ones—the ones who have made soul-destroying compromises, the ones who have spent their careers sucking up to someone they despised—who really hate whistleblowers. Those are the ones who think: Why can't those traitorous sons of bitches keep their big fat mouths shut like we do?

"Our lawyers were forbidden to ask: Do you think it was right to help enslaved people escape the South even though it was illegal? Do you believe that Jesus was right to throw the moneylenders out of the temple? The prosecution wanted to exclude anyone who read the *New York Times* or the *Washington Post*. Honey, it was insane.

"The craziest thing was that in a rare, let's say *singular* judicial decision, Dan wasn't allowed to explain why he'd committed the 'crime.' We were forbidden to explain how what we'd done was related to Vietnam. It was a huge relief when the case was dismissed, but also disappointing, because now the entire point of releasing the Pentagon Papers would be forgotten because some shady dudes broke into Fielding's office. That's why I agreed to testify before the grand jury, but only in open court."

What did *I* take away from that? Tony had called me *honey*. Why should that have mattered? Whatever he felt about me was so much less important than the trial. And *honey* was hardly a declaration of undying love. The cashier in the Martha Washington called Tony *honey*. My mother called me *honey*. Southerners called everyone *honey*. It meant nothing.

Maybe I was a little bit in love with him. But what did that even mean? There are so many kinds of love. Even now, when I say about Tony, "He was my . . ."—that's where the sentence ends. Maybe there is no word for what he was. Maybe I never knew what the right word was.

I thought about him more than I thought about my family or my friends. I talked to him in my head. I imagined long conversations with him before I fell asleep. I dressed more carefully, paid closer attention to how I looked when I was going to see him. I acted differently. More reserved. I was never entirely "myself." I was happy to see him when he showed up and disappointed when he canceled.

Yet we still hadn't touched, except by accident. He was not, strictly speaking, my boyfriend. I had no idea what I meant to him. His friend, his confessor. A listener. A pair of ears. A younger woman. A younger woman writer who was impressed by what he'd done.

I had no way of knowing how many people he'd told the same stories to, in the exact same words. Obviously, he wasn't telling me anything he hadn't said before. It shouldn't have bothered me, but sometimes it did. It made me feel as if I could have been anyone. He was telling me the most important things, but they were stories he'd tested on other audiences, stories proven to have an effect on his listeners.

I wondered if Tony thought that I might have a positive influence on his writing. But if that was true, why didn't he ask me to look at his book after that first night at Henry and Grace's? And why didn't I offer? I was afraid that his work might not be good, and then what would I do? It would have felt wrong to lie to someone who'd blown up his life for the truth. If his writing was bad, and I said so, that would have ended everything, though we'd pretend that wasn't the reason.

All the time I spent with Tony, I never once thought: I'll write about this someday. I'd never written about my life, or anyone's life, without the filter of fiction. But already I was interested in the turns that narratives took, in how stories played out and in the ways in which people told them. One of my favorite films was a short documentary, "Betty Tells Her Story," in which a woman recalls buying and losing the perfect dress to wear to the governor's ball, a dress that made her feel beautiful for the first time in her life—and that she left on the roof of her car when she drove away from the shop. She tells it twice, first as a humorous anecdote, the second time as the painful experience it was.

One reason why people are attracted to, and wary of, writers is that they hope, or half hope, that someday they'll read about themselves in a book. But they're also afraid that it might be an unflattering or excessively accurate portrait. People don't necessarily want to be around someone on whom nothing is wasted.

Tony asked me if there was anywhere special I wanted to go.

I said, "San Juan Bautista."

It's the mission where Judy falls to her death at the end of *Vertigo*. Except for the redwood forest, it was the one important locale in the film that I hadn't visited. I'd become like those tourists who go on destination trips to the sites they'd read about in a beloved bestseller. Emmet and I had walked all the way to the Mission Dolores graveyard that Madeleine haunts and, another day, out to the Palace of the Legion of Honor, where Scottie tries to make Judy admit that she's been there before, in her previous incarnation as Madeleine.

"Are you serious?" Tony said. "That's a hundred miles south of here."

"Maybe not. It *is* far." I didn't know why I'd mentioned it. The last thing I wanted was to go on a high-speed two-hour drive to the scene of the tragedy from which Scottie will never recover. A fan pilgrimage to the site of an on-screen death seemed ghoulish and cheesy, like leaving an impassioned love note on Jim Morrison's grave. Also, it seemed like bad luck.

"Let's not," Tony said. "It seems like bad luck. Hey, what's the matter? Are you okay?"

"I'm fine," I said. "I'm fine." I couldn't say: That's just what I was thinking! It might make him nervous to know that we were reading each other's mind. He was just paranoid enough to begin to wonder if I really was who I said I was. If I were a secret agent mentalist, why would I *admit* to reading his thoughts? Maybe to throw him off the track. I thought of the lonely guy I'd met in India whom everyone suspected of working for the CIA. Maybe he actually *was* an agent. Maybe his loneliness was an ingenious cover.

I was trying to write a novel, and the work was going so badly I can't even remember what I was trying to write. The first two books had been, in different ways, a pleasure. But now writing felt—as Tony said—like trying to chip away at a block of stone without having the tools. I worried that it was my punishment for calling myself a writer, for assuming I would always have access to something that could vanish without warning. The angel gives you a little kiss, then flies off to kiss someone else.

If the dry spell didn't worry me as much as it might have, perhaps that was because everything seemed so temporary. I wasn't planning on staying anywhere for very long, and if I went somewhere else—home to New York, say—things might be different. Sooner or later, I'd write something I liked. I don't know why I believed that my life as a writer would resume as soon as I went back East, but that was what I told myself, and it kept me cheerful.

I'd still never been to Tony's apartment. I knew that he lived on Lincoln Way, across the park from Henry and Grace. One night I gathered all my courage and asked, faux casually, if he was living with someone. He seemed shocked that I would think he'd be riding around with me, night after night, with someone waiting for him at home. He drew into himself, the way he had when I'd babbled on about Ellsberg's divorce.

Several days passed before Tony called and showed up again. When I asked what he'd been doing, he said that he'd been writing. Maybe if I'd paid closer attention I would have heard him say that he was *trying* to write. Maybe that's what he *did* say. He was *trying* to write, as was I. It's surprising that we so often talked about books and hardly ever talked about writing. But later it would make more sense.

Tony told me he'd read a lot in prison. It was easy to get books there. His lawyer was good at bringing them in, or smuggling them in, depending on the book. Tony had memorized whole pages of fiction, the way he did with Graham Greene, just to keep his brain from shutting down forever.

I said, "That's why I took German in graduate school."

"I wish I knew more languages," said Tony.

I asked Tony what he'd memorized. He said the section from *Gravity's Rainbow* in which two English women serve Slothrop a smorgasbord of disgusting British candies: gin marshmallows, gooseberry-clove tapioca confections, slippery elm and cherry quinine, pepsin nougat, rhubarb creams with a liquid center tasting of mayonnaise and orange peel. Tony rattled off candy after candy, sentence after sentence. It was the most carefree I'd seen him, except when he talked about the time he'd thought that he was going to jail. Mayonnaise and orange-peel candy! He threw back his head and laughed as we headed west on California Street. I liked the fact that a book—that *thinking* about a book—made him so happy.

I said, "What about that disgusting dinner party scene?"

Tony said, "Snot soup. Vomit vichyssoise. Wart waffles."

Sausage and blueberry pie.

That was our first conversation about *Gravity's Rainbow*. The novel could have been written for Tony. It shared so many of his obsessions: military engineering, intelligence gathering, surveillance, secrecy, weaponry, government lying, the demonic misuses of technology. In the last third of the novel, there's a song about paranoia.

The first time I'd left California to return to New York, I'd crossed the country by train. At the station in San Francisco, Henry gave me a copy of *Gravity's Rainbow*.

He said, "Give me your other books. I'll send them to you. *Gravity's Rainbow* has to be the only book you have with you. You can't have a choice. Just start reading. And if you can't figure out what's happening for two hundred pages, don't worry. Hang in there and you'll catch up."

I read it on the train. I loved it. For years, I thought of it as one of my favorite novels, but I have never reread it, and I wonder if I ever will. I remember admiring how it ranged from London during the Blitz across the nightmare landscape of postwar Europe, all of it leading back to IG Farben and the V-2 rocket. Along the way are vaudeville songs, dances, slapstick, flat-out grossness, characters with Dickensian names, mystical philosophers, mad scientists, Proust and Melville and Rilke.

Much of the book centers on the development of Germany's new stealth weapon. "A screaming comes across the sky" during the bombardment of London, where two groups of men are under enormous pressure, trying to figure out the secret of the newly destructive German technology. Underneath the chaotic, farcical, maddeningly self-indulgent surface is a history of Nazi weapons manufacturing and of the German scientists that the US brought over to work in our space and atomic energy programs. As a huge cast of characters muddle through an insane world, there are Brechtian songs, references to tarot and the I Ching, and a narrative voice that seems at once like the voice of the moment and of the centuries before and after.

Its publication was a major literary event, though it was never clear how many people read it all the way through. The literature committee voted to give it the Pulitzer Prize, but the Pulitzer board refused, and no award was given that year. When the novel won the 1974 National Book Award, the famously publicity-shy Pynchon sent, as his representative, a comedian, Professor Irwin Corey, a monologist, like a Beckett character with a thick New York accent, Einstein hair, and a string tie that looked like a knotted electrical cord. I thought it was the coolest thing a writer had ever done. Hadn't *Gravity's Rainbow* told us? Given the state of the world, hiding out and keeping your head down was simple common sense.

Tony moved through the Martha Washington as if he'd just kicked off uncomfortable shoes. He always took the table farthest from anyone else.

I suppose there were always signs that Tony was walking a

narrow and perilous edge, hints that I chose not to see. I should have paid more attention to his story about Esalen, but at that time, it was common for people to have a bad drug experience over the weekend and be back at work Monday morning.

Why did he save his most important memories to tell me in a seedy all-night cafeteria? His car was so much more private and comfortable. There were quiet places where we could have parked. Where we *did* park. But each time we went to the cafeteria, he mentioned that the room dimensions and the awful acoustics made it impossible to eavesdrop on its patrons' conversations.

Even state-of-the-art recording devices, he said, couldn't handle the clatter, the ambient noise. I wondered if that was really why he went there or if he just liked the sausage and pie. I understood why he didn't want anyone overhearing him. And I knew that there was still a chance that he was being watched.

The cafeteria's lighting pooled in places and faded in others. Tony sought out the darker corners. It made sense. The office of his friend's psychiatrist had been burglarized. He'd been followed and monitored and jailed. He felt safer in a public place where the acoustics were so bad that even I could hardly hear him.

What was he saying that could have gotten him in more trouble? He told me that in a locked room at RAND were reports so top secret, so highly classified, that they would make the Pentagon Papers look like Dr. Seuss. He said he had access to information that would indict and convict his former bosses and cut through the layers of bullshit under which his "superiors" (air quotes) buried the truth.

Tony could imitate his former colleagues at RAND—the math nerds, the chess champions, the rapacious white men. After a while I felt as if I knew what it was like to work at a place where the office and the social life ranged from tedious to soul-destroying to scary and enraging. No wonder Tony and Ellsberg were so happy to find each other.

Tony could do voices and accents, especially a range of Southern accents. He did a pitch-perfect Lyndon Johnson: "We are not about to send American boys nine or ten thousand miles from home to do what Asian boys ought to be doing for themselves . . . We need somebody to track these guys and whup the hell out of them, kill some of 'em, that's what we need . . . I can prove that Ho Chi Minh is 7yga son of a bitch if you let me put it on-screen . . . I know we oughtn't to be there. But I can't get out. And I don't want to be the architect of surrender."

Kill some of 'em. That's what we need.

There's a grim fun in listening to Johnson's recorded telephone conversations and Nixon's Oval Office tapes. The crudeness and vulgarity, the vindictive nastiness, the childish lack of impulse control shown by the leaders of our country—it's comical and terrifying to realize that these guys were in charge.

At one point Nixon tells Attorney General John Mitchell, "We've got to keep our eye on the main ball. And the main ball is Ellsberg. We gotta get this son of a bitch. Just because some guy is going to be a martyr we can't allow the guy to get away with wholesale thievery."

To which Mitchell offers a prediction based on his confidence in endemic American anti-Semitism: "All the people have to do is look at this guy on television and his name and so forth." *And his name and so forth.* Mitchell must have understood how well Nixon would parse the innuendos. The president bemoaned the "terrible liberal Jewish critique" influencing government policy. "Look at the Justice Department . . . It's full of Jews."

Nixon worried about "a wild orgasm of anarchists sweeping across the country like prairie fire." A wild orgasm. And he proposed a drastic but decisive plan for ending the stalemate in Vietnam.

"The nuclear bomb," he mused aloud to Henry Kissinger. "Does that bother you? Henry, I just want you to think big."

I didn't talk about myself anywhere near as much as Tony did. In fact I hardly talked about myself at all. I think that Tony would have listened, or half listened, to whatever I said. But nothing that seemed especially dramatic—or important—had happened to me, certainly not compared to what had happened to him.

I'd grown up in a brick house—I'd learned from "The Three Little Pigs" that this was the only guarantee of safety—built for a judge in 1920 in what is now the Ditmas Park neighborhood of Brooklyn. In the fourth grade, I'd switched schools and desperately tried to make new friends by boasting about the size of my house, and it had not gone well. I'd read constantly, indiscriminately, stumbling under the weight of books I lugged home from the public library. I was a good student. College. Graduate school, early marriage. Cambridge. Avocados.

India, there was that. Another thing that Tony and I had in common was that Asia had changed us. But my experience—books from the Bombay library, a balcony on the sea—was so unlike his immersion in a brutal war that those months in India hardly seemed worth mentioning. After hearing Tony's stories, talking about the joy I felt in the Colaba market would have seemed like reading aloud from a tourist brochure. Visit Southeast Asia!

Tony liked hanging out with a writer. Something about my life, or whatever he imagined my life was, must have seemed like proof that writing could be a job, a calling, that you could be reasonably respectable and pay the rent (or split the rent) without working for NASA or a villainous think tank.

I didn't want him to read my novels. They didn't seem trivial to me, but I was afraid that he might think so. They weren't *The Quiet American.* They weren't *Gravity's Rainbow.* My second book, *The Glorious Ones,* which was about to be published, was a series of first-person monologues spoken by the members of a fictional commedia dell'arte troupe in sixteenth-century Italy. Tony had seen war and torture. He'd been in prison, and what had I done? Written the last fifty pages of the novel, a monologue spoken by a dead woman, in a single night, high on speed, in a friend's sweltering Manhattan loft.

At the poker game he'd asked if I'd look at some of his writing, but he hadn't brought it up since then. I didn't want to ask unless he mentioned it. Several times he'd said that writing had always been impossible for Dan. Despite the fortune Dan got for his book, he couldn't do it. I wondered if Tony was talking about himself, except for the part about the fortune.

One night at the Martha Washington, Tony said, "No one in the Saigon office wanted to touch the crop-destruction program, though it was on the list of things that we were assigned to write up. If the military was doing it, we were supposed to explain that crop destruction was a whole different animal than defoliation. Defoliation was about denying the enemy shelter. Crop destruction was about starving kids. And both programs were successful beyond our most optimistic projections. No one wanted to put their name on *that*. It was tricky enough, putting a positive spin on our everyday war crimes. No one wanted to suggest poisoning *more* rice fields.

"I volunteered. My bosses were delighted. They'd read the writing on the wall, and it said, Tony Russo is going to fuck you. Writing the defoliation report was writing my own pink slip. By then, they knew that I wasn't going to lie, and if I wrote the truth, they would fire me on the spot.

"My good ol' boy background came in handy. I hung out at the bar where the helicopter pilots drank. The pilots thought I was a reporter. They had some idea that I could get their names in their hometown papers. They wanted Granny to know about all the good work they were doing over there despite what the hippies and commies said. Also they were impressed that a pocket-protector dude like myself knew so much about aeronautics that I could probably have gotten a real job as an airplane mechanic.

"One of the pilots took me up. Marty. He wasn't the whistleblower, so I left his name out of the report. I stole him a bottle of single malt from the RAND villa. I could have bought it on the black market, but I liked making my bosses pay. Marty was a good guy, popular. No one asked why he was taking a nerdy reporter for a joyride over the jungle.

"From a distance it looked like a shadow on the land. Then I saw that it *was* the land, the charred earth bristling with broken black toothpicks and slimy brown vegetation you could smell up in the sky. Some of the dead wood was bleached so white it was like flying over miles of broken bones. As a kid, we'd lived near a cabbage farm that got pretty nasty in late fall, and the swamp could get rank, but this was something else. Vegetable rot, spoiled eggs, gas-main explosion, battery acid, and a sweet sickly odor like burnt cinnamon toast. It scorched the back of your throat. There were patches where the rain had left neon-green puddles."

Tony dabbed at his eyes with a brown paper napkin.

"Marty knew it wasn't an ideal outcome. He said he didn't like killing trees. But war meant you had to kill *something.* Better trees than soldiers. Better trees than civilians. Marty should have written the report.

"I asked Marty, 'Where are all the people who used to live here?'

"He said, 'They brought in buses and moved them out of harm's way.'

"*Out of harm's way.*" Tony shook his head. "I wrote that crop destruction was counterproductive. It was making the peasants hate us even more than they already did. They would go without eating to feed the guerrillas fighting for their freedom. Their freedom from *us.* Meanwhile my bosses were saying, Hey, the Viet Cong have gone up into the mountains. They're planting rice up there, so we need to bomb the mountains, torch the rice. I grew up in farmland. You don't win hearts and minds by burning crops. I wrote the truth, of course. That was one of the two reports that got me fired."

I said, "What was the other one?"

"Torture," said Tony. "The other one was about torture. Can we not talk about torture right now?"

I was anxious and distracted when Tony didn't call, though he always phoned and showed up when he said he would. He was like a good boyfriend except that he drove too fast and sometimes talked too rapidly for me to follow and sometimes fell silent and sometimes cried and sometimes forgot that I was there. And the not having sex—what was up with that? I couldn't make myself ask if we were just friends or what? It would have embarrassed us both.

I sensed that Henry and Grace didn't approve of my spending so much time with Tony, though after Grace's warning, early on, they tried not to show how they felt. You needed boundaries when you lived on opposite sides of an interior wall.

Tony no longer came to the apartment. He waited for me outside. How we acted around Henry and Grace might have raised the question: Were we friends or a couple? The question never arose when we were alone.

If Henry felt that I'd stolen his friend, he never said so. He had plenty of friends. He knew that I would leave town, and that he and Tony would hang out again, without me. They still saw each other every so often. They met for coffee and went for walks when I was supposedly writing.

One morning, when Henry had been at his desk writing sci-fi porn and I'd been writing fairy tales that dead-ended after two paragraphs, we took a break.

The ritualistic way that Henry brewed coffee, one cup at a time in a French ceramic filter, was decades ahead of its time. We took our coffee outside and sat in the beautiful garden. I stared up into the fuchsia until my eyes went out of focus and the pink and purple blossoms hid the blue of the sky. I wanted to know why he and Grace worried about my being with Tony, but I didn't know how to ask, or maybe I didn't want to hear his answer.

Our coffee was half gone, then three-quarters gone.

"Henry, do you think Tony's . . . ?" I couldn't end the sentence. "Do you think Tony's . . . okay?"

"You should know," said Henry.

"I don't. I don't know."

One thing I liked about Henry was that you could watch him think. After a while he said, "Tony's had a hard time. Shoved aside by his celebrity friend. One problem is that the camera doesn't love him the way it loves Ellsberg. And no one wanted Tony spouting his crazy Marxist shit in court. That was *not* going to help their case. Tony's the one who's fun to hang with, the guy who has all the good stories, the guy who says stuff you don't expect. Ellsberg's people didn't want anyone doing *anything* unexpected. Supposedly Ellsberg and his wife were annoyed that Tony was named on the indictment. She wasn't going to shell out for Tony's defense. They needed him to step aside. They needed him to disappear."

"That's what Tony says."

"Tony's right," Henry said. "And how is that going to change? It's not. But that's not what's killing him. What's killing him is that *everything's* changed. And not in a good way. Even so, I'm pretty sure he'll be okay."

Henry knocked on the table. My coffee cup jumped. "The bottom line is, he's not in a room up there." He gestured up the hill toward the mental hospital. "That's the dividing line. If you're still down here, it means you're not up there. Yet."

I said, "Henry, you know that's not the line."

"I know," said Henry. "Believe me."

One evening, when Henry and Grace were out and I knew that I wasn't going to see Tony, I decided to read the tarot cards. I'd let Moira read them for me, in her loft, but I hadn't done it for myself, not for a while. I was still wary of the compulsiveness that had me asking the I Ching for permission to leave my apartment in Cambridge.

The cards that came up were eerily like the ones that had appeared in Moira's loft. Swords, the Hanged Man. The Tower. It was as if the cards were saying, Do we have to tell you twice?

Eerie things happened then. We saw coincidences as signposts pointing to . . . where? The age we lived in, the drugs we took, the things we believed—we were one step away from thinking we lived in *The Twilight Zone* and at the same time intensely aware of a very real war being fought on the other side of the world. Checking our horoscopes and reading Frantz Fanon? We were fine with the contradictions.

The day after Ronald Reagan was shot in 1981, Nancy Reagan contacted celebrity astrologer Joan Quigley, who, according to TV host Merv Griffin, had predicted the attempted assassination. From then on, the First Lady had Quigley on retainer, vetting important dates and presidential allies. Based on Gorbachev's natal chart, Quigley gave him a thumbs-up. It was another example of how the language and ideas of the '60s were—as Jenny Diski wrote—appropriated by the '80s and "dressed in clothes that made them unrecognizable to us." Our flirtation with the occult became standard taxpayer-funded practice in the Reagan White House.

• • •

Late one afternoon, when Grace was working at the dress shop and Henry was off doing errands, Tony showed up at our apartment. He and Henry had planned to go out for coffee, but apparently one of them got the date wrong. He asked if Henry was home, and I said no, but please come in. Tony seemed surprised and a little embarrassed to find that I was alone.

He said, "I can leave. I don't want to interrupt your writing."

"I'm not writing," I said.

In all the time I'd known him, ever since the night of the poker game, we had never been anywhere but in his car or in a public space. We had never been alone inside, in private.

It felt as if we'd just been introduced. I didn't know where to stand or what to do with my hands and feet. I didn't know where to tell him to sit. I didn't know how to walk across the room.

My bedroom door was open. My rumpled bed was visible from the living room. At first I wished that I'd made the bed, and then I was glad that I hadn't when Tony glanced at my bed through the open door—and kept looking.

I asked if he wanted anything to drink, and he said, "Coffee would be great. Please. If it isn't too much trouble. The strongest coffee you have. Please. Did I say 'please'?"

"Three times," I said.

Strong coffee had its own directive, a place where it wanted to be consumed: the kitchen and the dining table. Not the bedroom or even the couch. I was relieved, in a way. I needed a shower. But maybe I was misinterpreting. Maybe Tony had been staring at my bed for a reason. Maybe older guys needed a shot of caffeine before they got it on.

I made the coffee according to Henry's slow-drip method. It seemed to take longer than ever. When I brought our cups out,

Tony was already sitting at the dinner table, leafing through the I Ching. Earlier that day, I had given in and asked the oracle for a clue to what was going to happen between me and Tony. The verdict was not encouraging. It agreed with what the tarot had told me. Twice.

Tony picked up the pennies and cradled them in his palm. He had the soft, smooth hands of someone who has never done much physical work.

He said, "You really think this book can predict what's going to happen?"

"Not exactly. I think it can make you see things from another perspective."

Tony said, "My grandmother used to tell the future and get advice by opening the Bible at random. I knew a woman who used to do the same thing with a copy of *Jane Eyre.*"

"Same principle," I said. "Sort of. Would you like to ask it a question?"

"Sure," he said. "Let's give it a try. Let's ask it, What's going to happen in the next six months?"

I wondered if he meant happen to *him* or happen to *us.* I wondered if we would even be in the same city, if the oracle would tell us that we wouldn't.

I counted the heads and tails. I went slowly, for Tony, who frowned with fake concentration, then smiled and said, "Got it." I was embarrassed. He'd been an aeronautical engineer, and I was acting as if he'd have trouble calculating six lines.

There's something erotic about fortune-telling: the intimacy, the power, the fear. The trust. The seductiveness of competence, dealing cards, casting coins, gazing into a crystal ball, tracing lines on a palm. It's a performance. When someone is telling your future, and you believe in it, and who doesn't, the two of you are climbing together, slightly out of breath, scaling a mountain from which you may see the hills and valleys beyond.

I was conscious of Tony watching me as I wrote down his hexagram.

Darkening of the Light. My least favorite sign. Why was I surprised? The tarot had warned me. As always, the oracle tried to put a positive spin on it, but the title said it all.

"Darkening of the Light means injury . . . Not light but darkness. First he climbed up to heaven, then he plunged into the depths of the earth."

Tony fell silent for a while. Then he said, "Poetry, but also bullshit."

It took all my courage to reach across the table and put my hand over his. He slowly slipped his hand out from under mine. It said something, but not everything. Withdrawing his hand meant that nothing was going to happen now, but his deliberate slowness promised that it might, someday. The afternoon sunlight streamed in from the backyard, and I watched a few fuchsia blossoms drop onto the paving stones. It wasn't quite warm enough to sit outside, but the California light was lovely. Grace had bought red anemones and put them in a blue vase, and the sun shone through them, staining the white wall scarlet.

Tony said, "Here's where I ruin the party again. I don't know why. There's some really awful stuff I need to say. I don't know why I'm telling you this now. You look a little pale . . ."

"A little *what?*" It occurred to me that this was the first time he'd seen me in daylight. What did he see? That was the question I'd asked my husband. I didn't want to think of that now.

"Should I go on?"

I told myself: You're a writer. None of this will be wasted on you. I still didn't want to hear it.

"Sure," I said. "Go on."

"The second report I wrote was the one about torture. From the day I got there, I heard rumors. I heard that we were hanging prisoners by their thumbs, shoving their faces in water, giving them electric shocks, threatening to kill their mothers. The whole enchilada. I heard this one CIA guy liked to hang NLF cadres from trees and wrap piano wire around their dicks and threaten to cut them off."

Just when I'd thought we might grow closer, when we were alone in the apartment and my unmade bed was visible through the open door, Tony was talking about castrating prisoners with piano wire. I couldn't help thinking that he—or, to be more exact, his subconscious—was telling me something that made me feel embarrassed by the vague stirrings of my own desire. I asked myself: What kind of person was I? What was my idle sexual curiosity compared to what Tony went through? I reminded myself to keep things in perspective.

"We trained the South Vietnamese guys who did all the wicked shit while we stood around watching. There's always a film. There's always some guy who gets his buddies drunk enough to think that filming atrocities is a cool idea. They were holding this guy's head in a tub, and when he came up, he looked like he'd left his face in the water. Like his face was a glove he'd taken off.

"I used to tell the guys at RAND, 'You do know we're torturing prisoners, and it's not only evil, it's a tactical mistake. Word gets back, and more young people sign up to fight against us.' And the RAND guys would say, 'Gee, that's terrible, Tony. But it's not our job to fix it. You know what a dirty war is, don't you, Tony? Well, this is not the cleanest.'

"Every so often we'd get an intel report about North Vietnamese torturing the US POWs at the Hanoi Hilton. And the place would go apeshit. Rapturous joy! Those Viet Cong sons of bitches! Look what they're doing to our guys! We need to win this war! But it was always a little weird because we were doing it too. We tried not to let the local staff know, but they weren't stupid. If the military heard about something the North Vietnamese were doing that we *didn't* do, something so nasty and disgusting we hadn't *tried* it yet, well, what the hell, they'd get the South Vietnamese guys to road test it. See if it worked."

I offered Tony more coffee, but he shook his head no.

"The first guy I met, they'd hung him by his thumbs. He'd been a musician. I can't remember what he'd played. He said because his thumbs were broken, he planned to change instruments when he got out, and he asked me—through an interpreter—if I knew the music of Django Reinhardt. The guitarist who'd had his fingers welded together in a fire and invented his style around his injury. Django Reinhardt! Can you believe—?"

Please don't cry.

Tony cried as he described cruelty after cruelty. I didn't want to hear it, but he needed to tell someone. I did nothing, said nothing; I listened. He would have been startled if I spoke. Behind him Henry and Grace's bright living room spun like the camera in *Vertigo*, circling around Scottie kissing a living woman who morphs, mid-kiss, into a dead one.

"Are you all right?" said Tony. "You look a little peaked."

"I'm fine," I said. "I—"

"Did I say stuff that upset you?"

"I'm fine," I said.

Tony said, "You know what? Let's get off the streets for a while. You need to come visit me. We could hang out at my apartment. It's nowhere near as nice as this. It's small. It's a mess. But it's quiet. It needs some serious straightening up before I can have guests. I'll call you tomorrow."

Within the next decade, San Francisco would be gentrified beyond recognition. But in 1974, traces of Gold Rush seediness and Spanish-Moorish Art Deco were still intact and visible everywhere.

Tony lived in one of the Moorish-themed buildings. Let's call it the Alhambra. His dim lobby smelled of wet carpet and every dog who had ever lived there. A keyhole arch rose over the doorway to the mail room.

The elevator was lined with mirrors veined with black and gold. Tony leaned back against the mirror. His hands were in his pockets. He looked like someone getting ready to whistle.

Unlocking the door, he said, "Excuse the mess. This is the cleaned-up, sanitized version of its normal condition."

Heaps of laundry and shoes, soda cans and takeout containers littered the floor. There was hardly any furniture: a kitchen table, two chairs, a sagging pebble-fabric couch in the same putty-greenish-beige range as Tony's car, a TV, a mattress in the bedroom. A cinder-block-and-wooden-plank bookcase contained a haphazard assortment of books on Vietnam, Asia, revolution, history, and the works of Ho Chi Minh, Frantz Fanon, James Baldwin, Jane Austen, Dostoyevsky, Ishmael Reed, and Thomas Pynchon.

The place looked like wherever the Symbionese Army was keeping Patty Hearst, like a cross between a safe house and a graduate student's apartment. Not like a home, not anywhere meant to last. Nowhere you would miss or want to come back to. It didn't surprise me. I had sensed that Tony was not the domestic type. But I hadn't fully imagined the disorder—the squalor—in which he was living.

I knew he hadn't been in San Francisco for long, which explained the sparse furnishings but not the pieces of 8-by-11 paper covering every surface. He must have driven all those pages
up from LA or had them sent. There was paper everywhere:
stacks of paper, heaps of paper, towers of paper, sheets of paper
spread across the floor. In one corner was a shaky pyramid of
cardboard boxes stuffed with reams of copy paper. I told myself that there was something childlike about it, that it came
from the part of Tony that liked sausage and blueberry pie. I
told myself that his apartment was like the bedroom of a smart
kid whose parents have quit trying to make him straighten up.
During my first year at college, my half of the room I shared
with a roommate was so messy that she wrote an essay about it
for her composition class. That Tony was ten years older than
me, that a man in his thirties was living this way, added to the
wounded-outlaw quality I found attractive.

I pointed at a stack of paper tipped over onto the floor. "Secret documents?"

"Actually . . . it's my book."

Did he want me to ask to see it? Was that why he'd invited
me? *Should* I ask? It was up to him.

"Come sit over here, okay?" Tony gestured at the couch. I
tried not to think about how Emmet had said those words and
started what happened between us. "There's something I want
to show you."

I watched Tony search through files, manuscripts, pages
torn from magazines. He sifted through some papers until he
found a reprint from the *New York Times.*

I have it in front of me now. You can find it online.

The headline says: "Ellsberg Associate Proud of Role Despite His 'Messed-up' Life."

The piece was published January 17, 1972.

Written by Steven V. Roberts, it describes how Tony's lawyers filed a motion to dismiss the charges against him in the Pentagon case and explains that he had already spent forty-seven days in jail. It says that Russo, a thirty-five-year-old economist and engineer, admitted to helping Daniel Ellsberg copy the Pentagon study of the American involvement in Vietnam. His refusal to testify against Ellsberg sent him to prison for contempt.

Interviewed in a café in Santa Monica, Tony tells Roberts that he is proud of the stand he took. Sure, the case has "messed up my life . . . but what difference does that make?"

Actually, it seemed to have made quite a difference. Roberts reports that Tony is on unpaid leave from his job as a research analyst at the Los Angeles County Probation Department. "He admits that he is broke."

Tony, writes Roberts, is worried that his telephone is being tapped and that his friends are being watched. This is how the article ends:

> No matter what happens to the motion, the Pentagon papers have clearly changed the life of Anthony Russo. He now considers himself a committed, full-time radical. As he said in a statement the day he went to jail, "the community of resistance is growing and Daniel Ellsberg and I have joined it."

Tony waited till I finished reading the article. Then he took the clipping from me, refolded it, and gently placed it on top of a stack of paper.

"I never once said that my life was messed up. I told the guy that the case had messed up my life. That is not the same thing. You, as a writer, should understand that . . . not-so-subtle distinction."

666

"You're right," I said. "The headline isn't what you told him."

"Thank you, ma'am," said Tony. "He didn't even get the facts right. I'm not so sure about Dan and I being comrades in the community of resistance. And I didn't refuse to testify. I just wanted it to be public. Now you know why I need to write my own book. Why I need to tell the story myself."

It occurred to me that I'd been a sounding board for the stories that Tony wanted to put in his book. He wanted to try them out on someone. Not anyone. A writer. All right. That was fine. It meant that I was doing something, if not to end the war, then at least to help someone who'd tried.

Tony made Vietnamese coffee, an elaborate process with sweetened evaporated milk, and we drank two cups each at his little kitchen table. He stood up and came around the table and leaned down.

I stood. We started making out in the kitchen. Our mouths tasted like coffee and sugar, and when we drew back to catch our breath, we laughed. It was almost like that first easy, uncomplicated laugh after the poker game, a laugh that was about nothing but the surprise of attraction.

Tony stepped back to let me go ahead, and we went into his bedroom and took off our clothes.

I wish I could say that it was the kind of sex that is the answer to every question, the gift for which we wait, the fireworks ignited by every spark of curiosity, affection, admiration, every laugh, every glimpse of a body part, every twinge of desire. I wish I could say it was the kind of sex that makes you think that from now on life will never be the same, the kind of sex that makes you wonder how someone could know what you have wanted all your life, what you will always want. I wish I

192 • FRANCINE PROSE

could say it was the kind of sex that makes you think, Now I understand why we have bodies. I wish I could say it was the kind of sex that makes you think, This is why people leave their happy homes, this is why they blow up their lives to feel like this just once, or just once more. I wish I could say it was the kind of sex that makes someone say, I want to have your child. I wish I could say it was the kind of sex that makes you think how brilliant Nature is for attaching the survival of the species to something that feels like this. I wish I could say it was the kind of sex that makes you stop thinking.

But I can't say any of that. Because it wasn't. It was awkward. I can't remember why. Nothing fit. Nothing went where it was supposed to go. No one's mind was on it. No one's mind could get away from it. Nothing felt especially good. Every step was the wrong step, every move a clumsy move. We stopped and started. I didn't mean to . . . sorry . . . oops . . . I hope that I didn't . . . It wasn't abuse or humiliation; it wasn't a lack of control or consent. It was simply not-great sex. Nothing more or less. It happens.

There's a passage in Walker Percy's *The Moviegoer*, just after the narrator has finally slept with Kate, the troubled, unstable cousin with whom he has been in anguished love throughout the novel: "We did very badly and almost did not do at all. Flesh poor flesh failed us. Christians talk about the horror of sin, but they have overlooked something. They keep talking as if everyone were a great sinner, when the truth is that nowadays one is hardly up to it. There is very little sin in the depths of the malaise."

This wasn't like that. This wasn't what that seems to describe, which, I've always assumed, is impotence. This wasn't that. But even so, I borrowed *The Moviegoer* from the library and looked up the quote. The not-great sex in the novel was romantic, but this wasn't.

I recall feeling distant, as if Tony had left his body and traveled a long way off. I remember thinking that we'd been closer—easier and more companionable—riding around in his car. Distractions, doubts, and second thoughts got ahead of pleasure, ahead of any possibility of pleasure. I think we both thought, It's better than nothing, for now. It wasn't the kind of sex that makes you think: I will never in this lifetime sleep with this person ever again! It was the kind that makes you think that sex might improve over time, which can sometimes happen when lovers (was that what we were now?) grow more comfortable and less self-conscious.

I wondered if it was me, if it was my fault, if there was a different kind of woman Tony wanted, a different body, someone who did something differently. In *Vertigo*, Judy knows that she will never be the cold blond princess, the only type that Scottie will ever love. I knew, from the film and from life, that people get imprinted on a particular kind of person, a body type, a mouth, a forehead, a smile. Why was I so drawn to damaged oddballs with Southern accents? How could you know, the first time, what someone wanted in bed? No matter how well you thought you knew a person, you started all over again as strangers the minute you took off your clothes.

The advantage to being promiscuous, as I suppose you could say that many of us were at that time, was that we had a chance to learn what we liked and what we didn't. We learned that it wasn't always personal. The chemistry could be off. The moment in someone's life, the light in the room, the flowers on the pillowcase, the phases of the moon—any circumstance, any detail could make it go right or wrong. With someone else it might be different. Men who seemed bewildered by female anatomy figured it out or not, got married and had long and happy married lives.

Awkward sex was nobody's fault. A disappointment, of course, but so what? If you liked the person, there was always something to like. It was comfortable to lie naked under the blanket in the dark. Tony's apartment was overheated, and the mess of papers everywhere made it feel like a nest.

We didn't pretend it was anything more than it was. We didn't say, That was amazing! We knew it hadn't been great, and we were okay with it. Our friendship—or whatever it was—had never been about sex. I understood that now. I hadn't been sure before, but now I was.

After a silence, Tony said, "I always had the feeling that Dan had a nonstop sex tape playing in his head. It was like his brain was like a giant multiplex showing a porn film, a war film, a spy film, a love story, and he was always the star. He'd see a girl on the street and start telling you about all the girls he fucked. *That week.*" Tony laughed. "He'd tell you how many times they did it, where they did it, what positions, whatever."

It wasn't lost on me that we'd just had sex for the first time and that Tony's pillow talk was about Daniel Ellsberg's sex life. Butch Cassidy and Sundance. Why not? I liked the fact that Tony was a warrior for peace. And wasn't homoeroticism part of warrior culture? Maybe I would have felt differently if I'd thought that Tony was my future. Neither the sex nor the swerve to Ellsberg diminished my desire to stick around and see what happened.

Tony said, "Can you imagine anything creepier than telling people—me—that he wanted to meet hippie chicks? I think he would have fucked a Manson girl if she promised not to kill him. Or even if she wouldn't. I took him to a commune in Topanga Canyon where everyone went around naked. I thought his eyes would pop. He disappeared for two hours while I talked politics with my friends."

"Were they naked?"

"My friends?" Tony lit two cigarettes and passed one to me. He said, "You know, I can't remember. I remember they had the best weed. We were trying to end a war. Dan wasn't a rapist. Why should I care if he fucked everyone over the age of consent at the naked commune?"

"It doesn't matter." I wasn't talking about his friend's experience on the naked commune. I was talking about what had just happened between us, and I think Tony knew that.

He said, "There's a funny story. Who knows if it's true. When Dan was hiding from the FBI, he called his downstairs neighbor in Cambridge. Dan said he desperately needed a favor. Would the neighbor go upstairs—Dan told him where the key was—and get rid of the sex toys, the Kama Sutra, and hire someone to take down the mirror over the bed. I thought, Jesus, we busted five presidents for lying and took on a racist imperialist war, and his big fear is that some FBI dude will find his vibrator."

"Did the neighbor do it?"

"You bet. Dan can be very persuasive. You know the line that cracked me up? Apparently he told the neighbor, 'I wouldn't want anyone getting the wrong impression.' He didn't want anyone getting the wrong impression!"

Tony said, "We tried. We really tried."

At first I thought he meant him and me, but after a moment I realized that he meant himself and Daniel Ellsberg.

One dangerous thing about not-great sex is that it makes you miss the real thing. It makes you search your memory of the past for something better and then romanticize a situation you would probably still be in except that it was impossible. I didn't want to think about being with Emmet in our hotel room in Palenque, after we came down from the mushrooms.

Lying in the dark, that first time, Tony asked me what I liked about being a writer.

I thought, Okay. He's trying.

I said, "This book that's about to be published, I wrote the last fifty pages in one night. It's in the voice of someone else, a made-up character who died centuries ago. The words came pouring out, page after page. I stayed up all night, and by dawn the novel was done."

He said, "That sounds like a dream job, getting paid for hearing voices. I mean, something besides the voice of your own guilty conscience."

That was how we became not exactly a couple but something like one, an organism with tendrils reaching into a future, though we both knew that we were never going to wind up together. We made no plans beyond the next night. Neither of us had expectations. Neither of us was fooling ourselves or the other person. No one was jealous of former lovers. No one wondered who loved the other more, or if they were loved at all. No one was thinking about love.

Or maybe I was, a little.

Tony told me he'd been going to workshops around Los Angeles run by a sex therapist named Betty Dodson. Essentially they were about masturbation, though they called it something else. He couldn't remember the name. Maybe he was embarrassed. I wondered if he was trying to tell me about something sexual he wanted, but as he went on, I began to think that it was his way of telling me that sex was complicated for him, and that he was getting help.

I knew that later in the spring I'd have to go back to New York to do a few of the small things that writers did then when a novel came out. Sign books, give a reading, have lunch with my editor. I thought I'd probably stay in New York for a while. It seemed unlikely that Tony would join me.

The night I told Tony I'd be leaving was the first time we discussed the future. He said that he was coming to New York in the late spring or early summer because he needed to see his agent and find a publisher for his book. We'd meet up again in New York. I could show him the city. He was looking forward to it.

I spent my last two nights in San Francisco with him.

Two nights before I left, I assumed we'd go to his apartment, but we didn't. We drove around. We wound up at the Martha Washington. Tony seemed removed. He was friendlier to the servers than he was to me.

I understood. I was going away. No one likes to be left. My husband had called me once long-distance, only once, to make sure that I no longer loved him but mostly to make sure that he no longer loved me, a conclusion I could hear him reach as soon as he heard my voice.

Tony ordered sausage and pie. Maybe because I felt closer to him, I found his diet troubling, as if I were on the cusp of being responsible for what he ate. I reminded myself: You're leaving. It's too late to change anything now.

He said, "There's something I need to tell you. I mean about how it all began. I told you so much, and not that. I can't believe I left that part out."

He looked down at the unappetizing purple mess on his plate. "It was when I was with the Motivation and Morale project. My job was to interview prisoners and defectors. To find out what made them tick. I remember asking the guys at RAND, What good is this going to do the Vietnamese people? And they laughed and said, This is not about that, Tony. This is about getting funded by the government to do research and then getting more money to do more government-funded research.

"Prisoner AG132. That was his RAND classification number. He was the most important prisoner I interviewed from an informational and human standpoint."

I sat back. I drank my coffee and stared into the cup. I didn't

want Tony to see that I already knew the story that he was
about to tell me.

The week before, I'd gone to visit Moira at the Reno.
Her little son, Amos, had just climbed out of the sink, dried off,
put on his pajamas, and, kiss kiss, gone to bed.

We sat at the long wooden table and filled two glasses with
amber liquid. Moira knew about Calvados when most of us
thought that the height of sophistication was a Chianti bottle
wrapped with straw. Her voice was warm, roughened by cigarettes and a deep, throaty laugh. She asked if I was still seeing that guy the tarot warned me against. The whistleblower.
When I said yes, sort of, she asked if I was sleeping with him,
and when I said yes, sort of, she said, "Okay. Here's a crazy coincidence. You need to see this."

Moira had a film-editing machine (in those days they were
the size of jukeboxes) in her loft. Sometimes other filmmakers
rented it. Her former husband was editing a documentary about
San Francisco war resisters.

She threaded the film into the Steenbeck, and talking heads
flipped by. Tony's face appeared in close-up on the screen.

Moira said, "Isn't that your boyfriend?"

I said, "He's not my boyfriend."

Moira waited for me to say more.

"Well, there he is. Whatever he is."

It was strange to see Tony in my friend's editing room,
speaking to me and Moira and anyone who happened to be
watching her ex-husband's film.

The film had been shot in her loft. Tony sat on a high stool,
alone, dramatically lit. Henry was wrong when he'd said that
the camera didn't love Tony. The lens and the lighting adored

him. He looked radiant and happy. He tilted his head back as if he were scanning the ceiling for an encouraging sign, and he smiled when he seemed to have found one. He looked at once sweet and possessed, like a cross between a teddy bear and a Dostoyevsky hero.

He said, "Prisoner AG132 was the strongest, most courageous and spiritual person I've ever met. This was spring 1965. I'd been in Vietnam for three months. I was working in the National Interrogation Center, where they brought the most important prisoners."

Tony leaned forward. The camera zoomed in. I edged closer to the screen. He'd talked about the interviews, but I'd never heard him mention a prisoner by number.

"You would have thought he was a monk. A lot of them were like that. They had a deeply spiritual quality. He was an army officer whose specialty was education. Instructing young people. He'd been doing it since 1948, when they were still fighting the French. He traveled around, teaching theater to children and teenagers in the countryside until he was captured.

"We both knew that he was recruiting kids to defend their country. He taught classes and encouraged his students to write and sing songs about defeating the Americans and bringing peace to Vietnam. He was very committed and sincere. We talked for days. He taught me about his culture. Things they'd never dreamed of at RAND, things that no one told us at the orientation meetings. He told me what his family was like. He taught me about the people in the villages, who they were and how they saw the world. He told me how the French wiped out his village, which his people rebuilt, and how the Americans torched it again. He taught me that the Americans were there to build more military bases and to avoid losing face. He taught me that the Americans had never, for one minute, intended to help the Vietnamese establish a democracy. He made me understand what it means to be committed, how different it is from being indoctrinated. When you've been brainwashed, your belief falls apart under pressure or attack, but if you are truly dedicated, your faith never wavers.

"He intrigued me. I spent a lot of time trying to figure out who he was and what he stood for. He had been in jail for months. He'd been tortured and beaten and starved. He kept himself sane by reciting poetry and singing. There was a poem he recited that went like this:

"War cease the deadly game.
Let the frightening slaughter vanish.
Let the farmers walk their contented feet to the paddy field.
Let the paddy ears drink ecstatically the milk of the dew.
War cease. Let the prisons open their gates.
Let the sweet hands gentle the young hair."

The poem was several times that long, and Tony wept in a half dozen places. He couldn't say the word *heart*; he couldn't say the word *joy*.

"I understood then that these people were defending their country, their freedom, their villages, their families. Their lives. Defending themselves from being ruled by another invader. I'd thought that those people might be fanatics, but this guy wasn't. He believed that the Vietnamese should be free. He was a good guy. A smart guy. We became friends.

"And that was it." Tony smiled and shook his head, in wonder. "That was what changed me. That was all it took. That was the moment. Every whistleblower has one. Though that was only the beginning. The start of a process. It took years for me to get the full picture, to overcome my own indoctrination, to see through what our president and the guys at RAND were saying.

"The first time I read the Pentagon Papers, I thought, That's what Prisoner AG132 was trying to tell me."

Moira stopped the machine and said, "Your boyfriend hijacked the film. Now Nick's film is going to be about whistleblowers."

I said, "I thought you said it was about war resisters."

Moira said, "Nick doesn't know what the fuck he's doing. Ask the rich gym-toned slut he left me for. Ask her. She's *producing*. She's the one with all the money and the brilliant ideas."

Moira started the film again.

Tony said, "On the second day of our interview, he sang a song to me."

Tony sang the song. It was a strange performance, beautiful and intense. Tony had his eyes closed, and when I closed *my* eyes and listened, it sounded like a cross between the North Vietnamese prisoner's song and Emmet's Southern Baptist hymn as sung by Harold Melvin and the Blue Notes.

Tony began to cry again. The camera kept rolling.

A voice off camera said, "Is it true that you got married in the courthouse before the trial?"

"Sure." Tony laughed. His face was still wet. "It seemed like a fun thing to do. One of my many flawed decisions."

The voice said, "Like helping Ellsberg? Do you regret it?"

Tony said, "I didn't help Dan. It was my idea. Dan helped *me*. And I *don't* regret it. I'd do it again in a heartbeat."

Moira switched off the machine. "I get it. I mean, I understand why you're attracted to the guy. He's charming and brave. He's a hero. A believer. Weirdly attractive. But I don't have a good feeling about this. Something bad is going to happen. Not to you. To him. But I guess that if it happens to him, it happens to you too."

"I'll be fine," I said. I'd loved the version of Tony I'd seen on film. He told his story clearly and coherently, and he wasn't driving. At that moment nothing—no one—was going to warn me about him. No one was going to tell me not to be with him. Watching the tape, I'd felt proud to know him, proud to be the one he'd chosen to ride around with night after night, proud to be the one he was sleeping with, though it hadn't gotten much better after that first time. Tony was a zealot, but he was right. He wanted people to know what he saw, what he'd been through. He wanted to tell them the truth about Vietnam. He'd gone to jail because he wanted to say that people like Prisoner AG132 were human.

I stared at the purple stains on Tony's plate as he told me the same story, using the exact same words, the exact same phrases as he had on Moira's editing machine. He recited the poem the same way, sang the song the same way, wept at the same moments.

As I heard him tell the story again, the pride I'd felt watching him tell it on film was replaced by something midway between sorrow and irritation. It was painful, hearing something he'd said so often before. I felt as if I was getting the packaged, crowd-tested version of his life-changing moment, the edited, buffed-up, polished story of what had turned him around. I didn't know why it bothered me, because I'd long since accepted the fact that he was telling me things that he'd said before. *Whistleblow while you work.*

He'd saved that story for me to remember him by because he knew the power it had.

I said, "I saw you tell this story. This same story. On film. On Moira's editing machine."

"Moira?"

"My friend. She used to be married to Nick. The filmmaker."

"Nice guy, Nick. Did you like the film? I mean, my interview?"

I said, "You told the story the same way you just told it to me."

"So?" he said. "Why not? How many ways are there to tell it? What difference does it make?" He honestly didn't understand what my problem was, and then I didn't either.

I said, "Who were the first people you told?"

"Told?"

"About the North Vietnamese prisoner."

"I told Dan. I told Lynda and my wife. I mean my ex-wife. I told Nick. And now I've told you."

Tony was right: How many ways could he tell it? I was so young, at once so full of myself and so insecure that I resented not getting the unique, original, personalized version of Tony's defining moment.

The next night, my last night in San Francisco, Tony and I sat in his car parked at the edge of Buena Vista Park, not far from Henry and Grace's apartment. Over the past few years, there had been several high-profile murders in the park, besides which it was rumored that bloodsucking vampire bats nested in the trees. My friends warned me not to go there after dark.

Before Emmet and I left Mexico in different directions, we'd spent our last day and night in bed, in our hotel room in Mérida—so unlike the place where Tony chose to say goodbye. But for Tony and me to do anything else would have seemed forced and contrived. Whatever had happened—or not happened—between us, it was never about sex in dark hotel rooms.

I wanted to believe that Tony was sorry that I was leaving, and that was why we weren't driving around. Parked in one spot, we could see and hear each other without my worrying that we might crash or get pulled over for speeding. We could talk without the clattering, the rattle and hum of the Martha Washington.

That night Tony told me that this had been a complicated and difficult period for him. He'd been having a hard time. He wanted me to know that he was grateful, that I'd helped him more than I knew. He had begun to think that the only way for him to get through this stage in his life was to write his book, to become the writer he'd always wanted to be, to get it down on paper as lucidly as he could. It would be a kind of exorcism that would help him conquer or at least pacify his demons.

Ellsberg and the media had left him pretty radioactive, but he would find a solution. He'd been trained to solve problems, puzzles, and equations. He'd write the book and maybe do some broadcasting for a progressive radio station. Maybe he could teach somewhere like Reed. Maybe Henry and his friends could help him arrange that. Anyway he wanted to thank me for having been kind and patient. I'd listened to him and been nice to him and made him feel comfortable, talking. He said we should stay in touch, *really* stay in touch, not just say that we would.

Did I want to take a walk? His hand shot up toward the park.

There were gangs and vampire bats in there! What was Tony thinking? Tony had been in Vietnam, and I was scared of a grassy hill in the middle of the city.

Tony said, "Okay, then. Let's call it a night. We'll definitely get together when I'm in New York."

"Yes," I said. "Yes, definitely. Yes. Of course. See you soon."

My blind hope that I would start writing again when I returned to New York turned out to be justified. Back in the city, I wrote a story I liked, called "The Bandit Was My Neighbor," based on the two boys in my high school class who happened to share the same first and last names. I changed their names to Salvatore Giuliano, after the early twentieth-century Sicilian bandit and the subject of a brilliant Italian neorealist film by Francesco Rosi. In my story one of the boys was the notorious outlaw, and one wasn't. The old woman narrating the story had been in love with the shy, peaceable one who remained in the village in which they grew up.

I sublet a place in Westbeth, a subsidized housing complex for artists, located in a former Bell Telephone lab, in Lower Manhattan, along the West Side Highway. The rents were very low. Diane Arbus had killed herself in her Westbeth apartment in 1971, just three years before, and I thought about her every day that I lived there.

I was renting an enormous art studio on the roof. My landlord was a sculptor who worked with shiny chrome beams. Several of them were attached to the wall, jutting out at right angles. By the end of the sublet, my thighs were purple with bruises from bumping into his work in the middle of the night.

The sculptor was going home to Chile for a few months. He told me that Westbeth was crawling with cockroaches, but that thanks to his cleanliness and constant vigilance, there was not one cockroach in his entire home, not one, and he expected to find none when he returned. He was glad to be renting to a quiet young writer who didn't seem like someone who would be having a lot of parties. I was a little insulted by that and beginning to get a bad feeling about the sublet until he showed me, with great pride, that from the window you could look down into Merce Cunningham's studio across the courtyard and watch the dancers practice.

He said, "I don't think this is voyeurism, do you?"

"No," I said. "It's hero worship."

"I can see," he said, "that we are two birds of one single feather."

The first night I stayed in the loft, two gigantic water bugs emerged from the drain in the kitchen sink. I wasn't surprised. They scurried off in opposite directions along the counter and out into the loft. I knew they'd been planning their escape, listening for my landlord to leave. Everyone said that roaches were smart. One of them got away, but when I trapped the other in a corner, it rose up on its hind legs and waved its forelegs at me before I stomped it. I was trembling.

It was a beautiful loft. You could see the river from the same bank of windows that overlooked the Cunningham studio. And yet I felt a sort of ... temperature drop, an interior chill, a warning that the old terrors might be coming back.

Once again, my anxieties began to replicate and grow. They collected in the dim stairwell between my door and the floor below. To reach the loft, you rode an elevator to the building's top floor, then walked down a very long, very empty institutional-white hall and climbed another flight of stairs that dead-ended at my door. There was no reason to climb those steps except to get to my loft.

Every time I left, I checked first, through the peephole. On the way back, I ran up the stairs as fast as I could, as if I were being chased. I was often breathless by the time I unlocked my door.

One afternoon someone pounded on my door. I looked

through the peephole at a redheaded stranger in his thirties (I thought) with an angry (also red) face. The fish-eye lens shrank his eyes to pinpoints and made his nose look warped and broken. I asked him if he was looking for the Chilean sculptor, but he wouldn't answer and kept slamming his fist into the door.

I felt as if I'd been waiting for him, or someone like him, to show up. I felt as if I'd summoned him with my fear. I called downstairs and asked the doorman to please come up and find out what the guy wanted. I don't know if the police were called. I didn't want to make that decision.

After that, the staircase scared me almost as badly as Kirkland Street had, in Cambridge. It seemed to me that an old enemy had returned after hiding, barely concealed, in the walls of the subsidized artist housing.

When my sublet ended, I arranged to stay with a friend, a documentary filmmaker who lived with a group of roommates in a loft on the corner of Grand and Greene Streets. This was pregentrification Soho, where artists occupied spacious but drafty and often unsafe housing. The elevators were manual; you turned a wheel or pulled a rope until the edge of the car was more or less level with your floor. No one thought twice about illegally tapping into a neighbor's electrical line. In the winter we took turns sitting on the cast-iron stove, with the oven on low. No one had an intercom to buzz visitors in; you threw the keys down to friends in the street. Once, two large dogs got into a fight in the freight elevator, and one of the owners got bitten when he tried to pull them apart.

The neighborhood was noisy. It wasn't the sweet noise of the fishermen singing on the beach in Bombay, but loud, hard-edged New York noise. I loved it almost as much. A few doors down from us was an S and M disco called Frankenstein. The sound system hit the bass line so heavily that it thumped through our building until dawn, which was when the doll factory down the block swung into gear, stamping out plastic toys. In the mornings, the gutters were full of imperfect doll heads, bright and pink and bald.

During the time between my leaving San Francisco and Tony joining me in New York, I got three or four letters from him, handwritten on yellow legal paper. He wrote that he was working on his book. He told me things he'd forgotten to mention in San Francisco. He described a restaurant in Saigon where he ate lunch and dinner, sometimes daily, for weeks. He missed their grilled marinated pork chops! He had become such a regular that the owner worried about him. No one, she said, should eat so much meat. It was bad for the kidneys. She started making him special dishes with vegetables and rice. He said that was the difference between the shops in Saigon and the Martha Washington, where no one cared how much breakfast sausage he ate. It occurred to me that his diet might have been a request for some sort of intervention, a plea that I hadn't been astute or confident enough to hear.

He asked if there was a pho restaurant in New York. I said I would find out. There was one I liked on Mott Street, but I didn't want to go there with Tony. I imagined the photomurals of Vietnam bringing back painful memories, and Tony weeping and telling the owners something they didn't want to hear. He would make their hard work harder. I didn't like imagining this, since mostly, while we were apart, I remembered Tony's most appealing qualities and none of the moments that had made me uneasy.

I told him that he wouldn't be able to stay with me when he came to New York. I was a guest myself, and my hosts' hospitality had limits. Even though two of my roommates were making documentaries about the war, even though Tony was an anti-war hero, my friends didn't like their long-term guests having guests, and I didn't blame them.

That was fine, Tony wrote. One of his lawyers had a townhouse in Greenwich Village, and he'd asked Tony to stay there. Tony invited me to stay there with him. I liked the fact that he'd asked me, but I worried it could be awkward. If it were love, I wouldn't have cared. I would have wanted to be with him anywhere, any way we could, every minute we had.

I wrote back: Don't worry. We'll figure it out when you get here.

I wrote to Tony, inviting him to come to dinner at the Soho loft on his first night in the city. My documentarian roommates assumed that he was my boyfriend. I'd told one of them about him, and the word got around. It seemed too complicated to correct them. I let them think what they wanted.

Tony and I arranged to meet at his agent's office.

Let's call her Ellen.

Her office was on the top floor of one of the three-story walk-up buildings that still line parts of Greenwich Avenue. I was breathless when I reached the top. A skylight and the highly polished wooden floors made the sparsely furnished room seem at once warm and austere.

The receptionist, Violet, wore the kind of perfect little black dress I'd seen on chic young women in photos of *Paris Review* parties. I felt sloppy in my T-shirt and long Indian-print skirt. When I said that I'd come to meet Tony, I caught something in her expression. Curiosity, certainly. Interest. Was I imagining concern?

I could hear Tony's voice from behind a closed door. That is,

I recognized his voice, but his normally slow, soft, musical delivery sounded louder, faster, ratcheted up. I was still trying to decipher the receptionist's reaction when she practically vaulted across the room to knock on Ellen's door.

Ellen came out to meet me and quickly shut the door behind her. A pretty woman in her forties, she wore flare jeans, a green velvet jacket, a cream-colored silk blouse with a bow. She clasped both my hands in hers and smiled. I understood why Grace Paley would want her as an agent. She radiated kindness. I wished she were my agent instead of the one I had.

Ellen looked like someone who tried to make other people feel better. I sensed that she would be helpful to Tony and, by extension, to me.

The door was still closed behind her. She seemed edgy, all the more so because, I could tell, she was, by nature, relaxed.

She said, "It's so good to meet you. I've read both of your novels. I'm a huge fan." I didn't care if it was true or not. I appreciated her thoughtfulness.

"You're Grace Paley's agent," I said. "I'm a huge fan of *hers*."

"She's a genius," Ellen said. "I only wish she'd take a break from saving the world and write a few more stories."

Ellen opened the door, and for an instant, as she waved me through, she had the dazed, uncertain look of a parent only now admitting that a child's birthday party has spiraled out of control.

Tony was sitting cross-legged on the floor. His clothes were rumpled, his stretched T-shirt pulled half out of the waist of his corduroys. He'd replicated his apartment: the stacks of paper, the carpet of typed and handwritten texts. He must have brought the paper with him. How had he gotten it up all those stairs? He hated the fact that the Pentagon Papers had become a story about photocopying, but he was addicted to paper, typed and printed and copied.

Tony picked up a few pages, read a few lines, dropped the pages, then dived back into the mass of paper.

I knew that something had happened, that a break separated then from now, past from present, West Coast from East. Tony looked more or less the same, only a lot more unkempt. He sounded more or less the same, only more frantic. The person on the floor of his agent's office was not exactly the same person I knew in San Francisco.

That person had smiled and had confidence in his charm. This person wasn't smiling. My feet felt suddenly very far from my head, and the light shining in through the windows glittered and buckled in a way that reminded me of the moments just before I fainted in Bombay.

I eased myself into a chair.

"Sit down," said Ellen. "Make yourself comfortable."

I was already sitting down. She might have noticed me trying to hide the fact that my breathing had gotten ragged and shallow. The room lurched slightly out of focus. It was beginning to seem like one of those dreams in which someone you know is supposed to be someone else—yet part of you knows who they really are.

I saw Ellen looking at me. I wondered what she saw. A young woman whose boyfriend was losing it.

I wanted Tony to stop it. To get it together. It was 1974. You didn't sit on the floor the way people did in the 1960s. It was 1974. Freedom only went so far. You acted a certain way in a literary agent's office. It was 1974. You weren't free to invent a whole new world with all new manners and customs. You *didn't* have a better idea. The old ways of doing things worked. Not perfectly, maybe, but what was perfect? It was 1974. You walked into an agent's office with a manuscript in an envelope or a binder—or the promise of one. You were dealing with a product, not a plan to save the world, not a way to make amends for your role in prolonging a war. You were part of a chain producing a product, like sneakers or potatoes.

Money mattered, and in general, the acquisition of money—even in small amounts—required certain concessions and the strong possibility that you might be asked to at least partly betray your principles and ideals. If an older male publisher asked a young woman writer if she'd written her novel all by herself, she giggled and said, Yes, I did.

I'd become the kind of person whom Tony's lawyers hadn't wanted on his jury, someone who has sucked it up and compromised and thought that everyone else should too.

I knew that something had happened to Tony, but still I tried to convince myself that I was getting things wrong. Misinterpreting what I saw. Maybe I'd forgotten what Tony was like. Maybe he was always this way. He drove too fast, talked a lot, ate weird food. There was a reason why the director of Esalen had given him a list of therapists. Maybe I'd remembered the best things about him and forgotten the rest. Absence makes the heart grow fonder. Maybe it also softens the brain.

Everything might have turned out differently if I hadn't been so young and unsure of myself. Maybe I could have been more helpful to Tony if I had trusted myself, trusted the obvious. Or maybe I was still too taken by the romance of contradictions, by the idea that someone could be two things at once. A writer and a listener. A Marxist and a tarot card reader. An antiwar hero and a madman on the floor of his agent's office.

By *turned out differently*, I don't mean that I could have saved him. I mean that I might have acted more consciously and bravely—and that I would feel better about it now.

Tony looked up and saw me. He stood and kissed me on the cheek, then cleared a space among the papers and sat back down on the floor.

He said, "Okay, this is where I write about my first weeks in Saigon." He read aloud a passage about finding his favorite pho shop. It was a version of a story he'd told me, only less clear, less organized. He skipped back to a section about the Great Dismal Swamp; then, after more rooting around, found some disconnected sentences about poker at the RAND villa.

"We were supposed to lose. If we won . . . if we won . . ." He let the pages fall. "All the book needs is some structure, someone to break it up into chapters and pick out the good parts and put the best stuff together. Isn't that what an editor does?"

"Sort of," Ellen said.

She looked at me. I shrugged. Ellen was the grown-up. This was her office. She was supposed to know what to do. I was Tony's friend. I was whatever he'd told her I was. She was older. She was his agent. She was in charge.

I was embarrassed by my desire to distance myself from Tony. I was a writer, not just the girlfriend of an activist falling apart in front of her eyes. I had been to Harry's office in the Chanin Building. I'd been insulted by my publisher. I'd gotten drunk at lunch. I'd written two novels. I knew how people acted in the literary world, and it wasn't like this.

At the same time, because I thought of myself as a good person, and because Ellen was so obviously a good person, I wanted to make it clear that I cared about Tony. And I did. I cared deeply about him. I wanted distance and closeness at once.

Tony seemed to have forgotten us both as he sifted through the paper.

After a while he looked up again and saw me and blinked—a modified double take, as if I'd just arrived. He gave me a funny little salute and said, "I'll be done in half an hour, and then we can go meet your friends."

It reassured me that he knew we had dinner plans. Yet he kept searching through the pages, less like a reader looking for a favorite passage than like a puppy scratching for a bone buried in the yard.

God help me, I thought. God help us both. What do I do now?

I knew that Tony had a lot riding on this book. It was supposed to be the fulcrum on which his life spun and came to rest in a place that made sense. He would finally gain control of his own history. He would say what he hadn't been able to say before. The truth would well up from inside him, and people would read it and understand.

He'd been under pressure for a long time, but this was a whole new kind of stress. This wasn't riding around San Francisco at midnight. What happened here mattered. His book was lost somewhere in the pages scattered across his agent's floor.

He read silently, moving his lips, put the pages down, picked up more pages, read them, put them down, working his way from one corner of the room to the other.

He shrugged. "Obviously the reason I can't find the part I'm looking for is because it's not here. I didn't write it yet. I wrote hundreds of pages, my original report. It's classified now, locked away forever in the bowels, and I mean bowels, of RAND, so I'll need to rewrite them from memory. The captive soldier hung from his thumbs, Prisoner AG132, all the stories I put in the report, so I can get it back, by which I mean I can get back to what it was like to be in Vietnam, the silky air, the smell of sweet vinegar, the put-put of the scooters, the bright green of the paddies, those beautiful kids.

"That's going to be in the book too. It wasn't just the bad

guys in Washington, the monsters from hell at RAND. It was me. I'm going to include the fake report. I can re-create it from memory, the hundreds of pages that say the opposite of what I actually wrote, that say that we were winning, that say we needed to kill more, bomb more, bear down harder, stay longer, refuse to give up ever, not until we'd bombed all Southeast Asia back into the Stone Age. We needed to do whatever it took.

"I want you to think big, Henry." Tony was crying now. Ellen handed him a tissue.

"The fake report written and issued by my superiors with my name on the title page. Readers are going to have to take my word for it, because I don't have the original, which is, needless to say, highly classified. I'll have to include a facsimile, because the original went to the Pentagon with my name on it. The Vietnam Motivation and Morale Study. By Anthony Russo."

Tony's voice had risen so sharply that Violet poked her head in.

"We're fine," Ellen told her.

Tony looked up just long enough to grace each of us with his familiar, winning, semi-mystified smile, then went back to shuffling pages.

"That's what it says here: 'Written by Anthony Russo.' And not one word of it by me. The not-by-me report was taken seriously, implemented by the Pentagon. So when I'd go to protests and I'd hear people chanting, 'No more genocide in my name, no more genocide in my name,' and I'd think, You know what? I'm the only one in this crowd who actually *has* had actual genocide committed in his name. His actual name! By Anthony Russo. They pretended that I wrote that torture worked, that deforestation worked, that the North Vietnamese were scared shitless, that they were a bunch of terrified little girls on the edge of mass surrender. You folks at home, you can start setting up the bleachers for the victory parade! That's what I supposedly said.

"And when I went to Dr. Strangelove and pretended not to get it, pretended I didn't know what happened. Maybe there had been some mistake. Dr. Strangelove dragged on his pipe, did that evil-eyebrow thing, exhaled a perfect stream of expensive French tobacco and said, 'Mr. Russo, you are officially terminated starting at the end of this meeting. Your service is no longer required. We can give you six months to go back to Santa Monica and tie up loose ends and keep your mouth shut and tell everyone you're leaving for unspecified health reasons. We can talk about severance pay. Or I can call security now. That is your decision. The security crew here in Saigon, as you may know, are not necessarily from our culture, nor are they always governed by our social norms.'"

Tony always could do voices. A deep baritone with a cultivated foreign accent was telling him to get lost or risk being beaten up by the guards. Tony had become his boss. Arch, imperious, malevolent. It was scary. Then he went back to being Tony, and he began to cry again.

"It was like a movie, like some James Bond nightmare, except that it was real life."

Tony stopped. He looked at Ellen, then at me.

Ellen said, "That's amazing. And terrible. That's the story you need to write, Tony. Just like you told us now."

Thank God she's here, I thought.

"You both know how the story ends," Tony said. "Except that it's still going on. They'll kill me if I publish half of what I just said. They'll lock me up again."

"We won't let that happen," said Ellen.

• • •

The fake report was, I think, among the most painful chapters of Tony's story. That speech in Ellen's office was the most coherent version of his experience that I'd heard so far. The fact that they'd issued a dossier of lies under Tony's name seemed like new information, though when I looked back, I saw how many times he'd tried to tell me and I hadn't understood.

I remembered him asking if my published novel was the same book I wrote. I'd dismissed it as a question from someone with no idea about what editors did. I'd chosen to forget that Tony was a serious reader. I'd chosen not to hear what he was saying. Seeing your name on an argument for endless war could certainly trigger a massive case of writer's block. He'd told me as much, but again I hadn't understood. Why hadn't I convinced him to show me his book? Why was I such a bad friend? Maybe I could have helped. At least I could have tried. I remembered, with shame, telling him that he needn't write chronologically. How clueless I must have sounded. As if *chronology* were the problem.

I hadn't been brave or generous enough. I hadn't thought it was *my place*. I hadn't wanted to pry, to assume too much. He was an antiwar hero. I was just a novelist. I was ten years younger. I should have done more. I should have been braver. What was I afraid of?

It's hard now to understand how much time it took me to acknowledge how serious things were with Tony, just as it's difficult to believe how long I managed to convince myself that it would pass. I gaslit myself into thinking that I was exaggerating, that he wasn't really having some kind of . . . what? What to call it? It was strange, being a writer, and, when it really mattered, coming up against the limitations of language.

"Your friends?" Ellen said.

"What?" I said.

"Tony said you're having dinner with friends?"

"Oh. My roommates. Eight of us live in a loft on Greene Street. I'm just staying there, really."

Ellen looked relieved. Was she concerned about my spending the night alone with Tony? I'd spent plenty of time alone with him in San Francisco. But he was different then. Did she know that?

How long had she known him? How had she become his agent? Those were perfectly normal questions, but I didn't know how to ask, not with Tony there. I was looking at Ellen over his head, over all that paper. I didn't know when she'd seen him last, if this had happened before. Henry and Grace had tried to tell me something that I'd refused to hear.

I'd never seen Tony around anyone on whom his future depended, someone whose approval he needed. But he'd stood up to cops and lawyers, FBI agents and judges. He'd gone to prison. He'd been beaten. He was unlikely to crumble around a friendly downtown literary agent.

"Some of this is stuff I wrote," he said, "and then there are documents, like I said, pieces of other people's essays, I can't remember if I included them in or not . . ."

He stood and put his hands in his pockets.

"I see," Ellen said. "Look, I've got to go. I'm sorry. Where are you guys eating?"

"There's a dinner at the loft where I'm staying. Didn't we just say that?" In fact I didn't know if I'd said it or just thought it.

"You did," she said. "You did say that. Excuse me. My mistake. Well, good."

She got up and came around her desk and hugged Tony. Then she walked over and hugged me. The hug lasted a beat too long. I could tell that she was worried.

"See you tomorrow," Ellen told me.

"Tomorrow?"

"At Tony's press conference."

"His press conference?" It was odd that he hadn't mentioned it. But I could see how that could happen. We hadn't spoken since San Francisco. We'd communicated by letter.

I assumed he would tell me about the press conference, whatever it was. I assumed he'd want me to be there.

"Quite a few reporters have signed up, Tony. Are you sure you want to do this?"

"What's *this*?" I was hurt and surprised, but why? He'd come East to do business, not to be with me. Despite everything, despite the worrisome changes I saw in him, I was proud to be with a person who had done something brave enough to make reporters still show up, years after the brave thing he'd done.

Tony said, "There's part of the story that's never come out. It's a hand grenade. I think it might be time to pull the pin." He pitched an imaginary bomb out the window, whistled through his teeth, said "Blam!" and grinned.

It wasn't the moment to ask what the hand grenade was, exactly. I could ask later. I wondered what Tony had said to make reporters curious.

Tony gathered and stacked the pages.

Ellen offered him a cardboard box big enough, she said, for a dorm-room refrigerator. She had the receptionist bring it up from the basement and assemble it while we watched.

Tony offered to help, but Ellen said, "Thanks, Tony. Violet can manage."

We watched Violet assemble the box, graceful and competent in her little black dress and heels, without a stumble or wasted motion.

"Thank you, Violet," Ellen said. "Violet's a miracle."

Tony could store the papers with Ellen until they figured out what to do next. All four of us helped fill the box, taking turns, scooping up handfuls of paper, gently lowering them into the box.

First Tony thanked Ellen; then I thanked her.

"No," she told me. "Thank *you*." She meant that it was my turn to deal with Tony. She was handing him over.

Tony bounced down the stairs before me and was waiting for me on the street. We sat on the front steps to talk.

He said, "I hope that Ellen understands that we're talking about a work in progress."

His voice was calm and musical. He'd slipped back into his easy, cadenced rhythm.

He said, "Ellen's a cool person. She's worked with political people before. She knows it doesn't come easy for us. She knows we're better at talking than writing. More comfortable with the microphone than the typewriter. Dan has a contract to write a book. I hear he can't begin."

He'd mentioned Dan's book contract before. It seemed like a sign that his former self was still inside the person who had been sitting on Ellen's floor.

"I think it was helpful for her to know I'd written those long reports, which at least shows that I can write. I can organize my material better than she saw today. I'm working in a new form. No one finds it easy. Pynchon wrote a couple of shorter books before *Gravity's Rainbow*."

"That's right," I said. "No. I mean, yes."

Maybe I'd overreacted. Maybe Ellen was used to writers acting unhinged. Maybe many of her clients were radicals worn past the breaking point by their long, discouraging struggles. She and I knew who Tony was. A whistleblower, an antiwar hero, a reader of *Gravity's Rainbow*.

Tony laughed at himself, a little ruefully. I laughed too. Rueful seemed about right. Rue was milder than shame. Everything could be fixed. He could go back to Ellen's tomorrow and have a sensible conversation about a contract and an advance. He could blame what happened today on jet lag. Maybe it was true.

The sky was a bright blue with tendrils of cotton candy pink creeping in at the edges. I thought of the fuchsia in Henry's garden. Was it still in bloom?

Tony said, "Sometimes you get this light in New York, this time of day, this season. Almost a Southern light. It's the pink of the magnolia in the backyard where I grew up."

"Let's go," I said. "We need to start walking. We're already late."

He took my hand as we headed southeast on Greenwich Avenue. We'd hardly ever walked in San Francisco. Our walks there had spanned the distance between his car and the Martha Washington, through the sketchiest parts of the Tenderloin.

We'd never held hands before. His skin was soft. His grip was neither too tight nor too slack.

In the balmy air, the sweet damp light, the fragments of conversation floated toward us on the breeze. As we turned onto 7th

Avenue, the sighing brakes and musical horns sounded as lush and propulsive as the *Vertigo* score. I felt lucky to be alive. I wasn't about to ruin the mood by asking Tony, What was *that* about? What the hell were you doing, back there in Ellen's office?

He'd always been anxious about writing. His fears had boiled over in a torrent of paper. He wasn't exactly an organized person. I knew that about him already.

Here we were, walking down a city street, doing something perfectly normal that we had never done before. Walking, just walking. Maybe things would be better here than they were in San Francisco. Calmer. Less frenetic. Tony wasn't driving. I would have more control. I knew the city. I'd grown up here. I knew how to get around.

After a while Tony leaned close to me and said, "You *do* understand why I wrote you letters? Why I couldn't call? You do know that my phone is still being tapped."

"I do," I said. "I mean, I figured that." I wasn't sure if I did or not. I didn't doubt him. Everyone knew the FBI eavesdropped on a range of people, often for no reason. It was government business as usual. The plumbers' orders to break into Ellsberg's psychiatrist's office had come down from the top.

But Tony used to phone me at Henry and Grace's. He hadn't been worried then. And why would the FBI care if he called *me*? What could we say that might sound subversive?

He said, "Did it look like my letters had been opened?"

"No," I said. "I don't think so."

It hadn't occurred to me to check. Was I sensible or naive not to look for evidence and clues?

Not long ago, I talked, on the phone, to a friend whose illness makes him hallucinate. We spoke for half an hour, and only after we hung up did I realize that most of what he told me couldn't possibly have happened. I wonder if I am unusually slow to figure out that something may not be true, if it has something to do with being a writer, with having worked so hard to make my readers suspend *their* disbelief. Maybe I'm overly trusting. It was complicated with Tony, because so many of the things that happened to him were at once extremely unlikely and matters of public record.

A few blocks from Ellen's, he stopped in the middle of the sidewalk. It was the golden hour, lit by the salmon glow of the Hudson. People were streaming out of their apartments and offices and racing to get the good tables at the bars along 7th Avenue. I understood why they were annoyed at us for blocking their way.

"I'm sorry," I told strangers. "Sorry."

Tony said, "They were on the plane from San Francisco."

"Who was?"

"Kissinger and Ehrlichman. In business class. Of course. At taxpayer expense. The way you could tell the higher-up CIA guys was that they flew business. Dr. Strangelove flew first. Anyway, on the flight here . . . every so often Kissinger would stroll into coach and shoot me a dirty look. I'd met him a couple of times. He was a friend of Dan's until he wasn't. Until he said that Dan should be executed. He'll probably be Dan's friend again. They'll kiss and make up at some formal dinner. They won't want to rock any boats. Especially if those boats are yachts. Redact that last part, okay? I don't want to sound bitter."

"Wow," I said. "That's amazing. What a coincidence."

"What is?"

I pulled him into the recessed doorway of a shuttered pharmacy with soaped-up windows.

"Kissinger and Ehrlichman being on the plane."

Was it true? It could have been. Did they fly commercial? Also improbable, but possible.

"Not really such a coincidence. Kissinger visited me in Santa Monica. He arranged to meet on a bench in a park near my house. Secret agent theater bullshit. He told me what bench to wait on.

"He tried to persuade me to swear under oath that Dan wrote the whole seven thousand Pentagon Papers as a plot against the US government. Was he kidding? No one would believe it. Henry was wasting his time. He told me I'd been stupid, wrecking my career for nothing. If I'd just been patient, the US would have left Vietnam in a few years. That was what he'd always said. We were never going to stay forever.

"I asked how many Vietnamese would die before we got around to leaving, and Henry said, 'Many unfortunate and regrettable things are bound to happen, Tony.' In that spooky Dracula accent. I thought, *This* is the real Dr. Strangelove. Compared to him, my boss, *my* Dr. Strangelove, that motherfucker was Mother Teresa."

Would Henry Kissinger really have met Tony on a bench in Santa Monica and asked him to pretend that Ellsberg wrote the Pentagon Papers? The chances seemed awfully slim. I couldn't run a reality check, because the reality around us included fast-moving traffic. I had to keep us headed in the right direction.

"Let's keep walking," I said. "We really are a little late."

"A little late is better than a lot late." Tony smiled, and something of the old charm shone through.

I couldn't afford to be anxious. I was responsible now. I was the one who knew how to get where we were going.

We needed to cross 7th Avenue. Taxis were speeding to catch the green light. Tony looked admiringly at them and then back at me.

He said, "If this book thing doesn't work out, I can drive a cab in Manhattan. It looks like a blast."

Then he stepped off the curb into the path of a taxi that swerved around him, honking wildly.

He scrambled back onto the pavement. My heart slammed around in my chest.

He wasn't even breathing heavily. He said, "Christ, did you see who was driving? Did you see who was driving that car?"

"No," I said. "It was a taxi."

I waited. Nothing he was going to say after this was going to be good news.

"Defense Secretary Schlesinger. He was coming straight at me. He would have killed me and kept going, and he would have gotten away with it. Hit and run. One more dead body. Who cares?"

"It was a taxi," I said. "Tony. It was a taxi."

"He was undercover. Obviously."

Was Tony joking? He wasn't. He wasn't the guy in San Francisco. He was the guy in Ellen's office. He was that guy and then some.

Soon we would be passing the St. Vincent's emergency room, but I didn't feel up to suggesting that we stop by the ER and check things out, just to make sure everything's okay, that everyone is . . . you know, feeling okay, and then we'll be on our way.

I dreaded dinner with my roommates, with Tony in this condition, whatever *this condition* was. But I was glad to be going to the loft. Someone would know what was happening. Someone would know what to do.

There were eight of us living in the five-thousand-square-foot loft. Seven rent-paying roommates: four documentary filmmakers, two architects, a lawyer—and me. One of the architects had put up the sheetrock that divided the space into bedrooms, an editing room, and a kitchen with a twelve-burner cast-iron stove and a table that seated fourteen. Everyone except the lawyer was a decent cook, creative with lentils and pastas and stews, a range of cheap, delicious dishes that could feed a crowd.

If the loft had rules, they were practical and unspoken. It was important to be on time for meals, not because punctuality was a virtue, but to keep from making things hard for the cook and to prevent the food from getting overcooked or cold.

My friends were annoyed when Tony and I arrived half an hour late. They glared at me when we walked in. I was sorry, but surely they would forgive me if they knew about our afternoon in his agent's office or about Tony thinking that the secretary of defense had tried to run him down in a taxi.

I still told myself that these might be passing aberrations, like ministrokes. The troubled but basically sane person I knew in San Francisco would emerge and pull the real Tony out from under the mask of delusion and derangement.

I introduced Tony to the group. No one seemed to blame *him* for our being late. Everyone said how glad they were to meet him, how honored, how much they admired him. I could tell he was happy to hear that. I remembered him saying he disliked it when no one at Esalen knew who he was.

"My pleasure," he said to each of them, dipping his head as he shook their hands. A faint echo of the smart, modest, charming Southern boy crept back in his voice. It didn't take much of that to win the others over.

Even so, the architect complained: The food was drying out in the oven.

One of the filmmakers, Iris, the best cook, had made a delicious lasagna, not dry at all. She dished out generous portions.

When Tony got his plate, he said, "Could I ask one of you folks a favor? Would someone taste this for me?"

"Are you allergic?" asked the architect.

"Not as far as I know," said Tony.

"Is this an AA thing?" Iris said. "There's no alcohol in it, I promise."

Tony said, "It's not that. It's not that I don't trust you. But . . ."

It took us a moment to understand.

The lawyer said, "Are you suggesting that someone here would try to poison you?"

Tony laughed. "Not exactly. But there have been attempts to poison me. In the LA County jail, needless to say. Earlier too, in Saigon. So I don't trust anyone, not even my mother. I make my mom taste the food when we go out to eat."

Everyone was staring, first at Tony, then at me, to see if my reaction would help them figure out how to respond to a guy saying he'd let his mother take poison for him, if she wasn't trying to poison him herself. He'd never asked me to taste his sausage, his blueberry pie, or his lobster.

"I'm joking," Tony said. "Joking." But he wasn't laughing. Nobody was.

Joking about being poisoned by your hosts was rude. It wasn't something you said. Tony and Dan used to talk about the culture of timidity at RAND, but by 1974, it was everywhere. You knew what to say and what not to. You knew what jokes not to tell. You didn't ask your hosts to taste your food.

I was sorry he'd said it, but relieved. It was helpful to see, on the others' faces, the realization that something was . . . off. I wanted to let them know that he hadn't been like this in San Francisco, but no one would make eye contact with me long enough for me to communicate something so complex.

Anyway, except for the hiccup about the food, which no one

tasted for him and which he ate and said was delicious and asked for seconds, he couldn't have sounded more reasonable, more well-informed. More sane.

That is, if you overlooked the fact that he spoke for twenty minutes nonstop, hardly taking a breath, on the subject of poison. Since the subject had come up . . . well . . . he knew about lethal doses, a history that went back to the Egyptians and the Borgias and up to the latest KGB and CIA secret assassinations. He said that he had a high school history teacher who said the apple in the Garden of Eden had been laced with Egyptian poison. I'd heard that story before. It was comforting, in a way, or at least it reminded me that Tony could tell coherent stories.

I think my roommates expected him to talk about the Pentagon Papers. Inside information, political gossip—that was probably what they'd wanted. They had questions. But covert assassination was interesting enough. They were content to hear him say that you could trace the ways that toxins were administered by the KGB back to the Renaissance and beyond.

I said, "Tony, have some more lasagna. Tony started out as a scientist, that's why he . . ." No one seemed to hear me.

He said, "They tried to poison me at NASA. I'd thought that people liked me there. But one day at lunch my burger tasted funny, and when I asked my friend to smell it, he said, 'Smells like rocket fuel.' I puked for a week. Sorry, I know we're having dinner. Then at Princeton it was just your standard-issue cafeteria food poisoning. Or so they said. No one else got sick. But the shit really hit the fan, so to speak, when I got to Vietnam. It started when my bosses figured out that we didn't see eye to eye on certain things. Like the truth. What broke my heart—and nearly killed me—was my local pho shop. I loved that place. I wanted to think they loved me back. I don't know what the guys at RAND or the CIA paid them, how they threatened them.

But one night after dinner at the pho shop I went home and looked in the mirror and my lips were blue. The pho had had a funny taste, like almonds. Cyanide, but not enough to kill me, probably not as much as they'd been told to put in my soup. I'd thought they'd cared about me. They were like family. But they had kids. And fear works wonders. I guess they saved my life by not giving me a lethal dose. I had to go to the hospital, where they said I was lucky I'd survived."

The lawyer said, "I didn't think that someone could survive cyanide poisoning. I was under the impression . . ." His voice trailed off. No one liked him very much.

Tony said, "I'm here to tell you that it's possible. I'm living proof. Me and Rasputin, except that they finally got him, and I'm still walking and talking."

I said, "Speaking of poison . . . why don't you tell them about the defoliation program?"

I sounded like a pushy mom. I didn't care. I wanted to urge him toward a more important or more plausible subject. Even if he cried. The others would be crying too when he described the ruined countryside.

"Yes," Iris said. "Tell us about that."

Tony looked at me, the first dark look I'd ever gotten from him, shot through with resentment, the look of a child whose parents are nagging him to perform.

He said, "If it's all the same to you, to quote my friend Bartleby: I would prefer not to. Everyone makes mistakes. You seem like nice people, and I don't want to burden you with the weight of my brilliant career as a war criminal."

He shrugged. No one said, You weren't a war criminal! No one said, You were the one who tried to expose the genocide! No one said, You were a hero! No one said anything. No one knew what to say.

"Meaning what?" the lawyer said.

Tony closed his eyes and shook his head. "It's way too dark. You can understand my not wanting to go back into a nightmare where it's all shadows and children with guns materializing out of the darkness and exploding palm trees and the smell of scorched—"

Tears welled up in his eyes.

The others looked at me. Their faces said: You brought him here. Do something.

They weren't going to help me. They didn't know what to do either.

They respected what Tony had done, the risks he'd taken. But they had their own worries, their own lives. They didn't know him. This was no longer the 1960s, when people like R. D. Laing were arguing that sanity and mental illness were just constructs. It was 1974. The psychiatric hospitals were beginning to discharge their patients onto the streets, and you learned that it was safer to keep your distance.

I looked from one of my roommates to another, and they looked away.

I don't remember how long the dinner lasted, or what else Tony said.

I invited Tony to stay the night. I was worried about him walking alone in a city that still seemed dangerous. Soho was deserted after dark. I felt responsible for him. I didn't mean I wanted to have sex, and he knew that. He was beyond that, anyway. He thanked me, but he said that he knew the way to his lawyer's house. It wasn't far. He had to rest up for the press conference tomorrow.

We waited for the elevator. Sometimes you could ring and ring and the people downstairs, who'd forgotten to send up the elevator, wouldn't hear and you had to go down the stairs and retrieve it. But tonight it groaned in a way that meant it was on its way.

"What are you going to say at the press conference?" I asked. "Can I have a . . . preview?" I remembered him telling me that he had access to documents that made the Pentagon Papers look like Dr. Seuss, and I wondered if this announcement of his would involve something that secret, that explosive. At Ellen's office, he'd called these new disclosures a hand grenade. Maybe that was why he was acting so strangely, so unlike his former self. Maybe he was just nervous.

"Let it be a surprise," he said. "A big surprise for everyone. Including you."

He told me the address again and reminded me that the event began at ten. His solid grip on the time and place seemed like a positive sign.

"Please," he said. "Be there. Okay?"

"Of course," I said. "I will."

When the elevator came, he kissed me goodbye, a peck on the lips. Then he gave me an equally brief hug, got on the elevator, and smiled at me as the door closed.

That evening my roommates took me aside, one by one, and said it was none of their business, but was Tony in some kind of trouble?

I said I thought so. Maybe. Yes. I didn't know. I said I was trying to figure it out. I said there were other people—his lawyer and his agent—who knew him better than I did and would have a better idea about what to do.

I told my roommates I was tired. I helped wash the dishes and went to bed. But I hardly slept.

I loved pregentrification Times Square. It still seemed like a foreign city, exotic and seamy, more like Tangier or Marseille than midtown Manhattan. If America was a melting pot, this was where the stew bubbled. It was strange that I, so anxious on the leafy streets of Cambridge and in my Westbeth loft, should have felt so at ease in a neighborhood that, in the minds of many Americans, symbolized crime and sleaze: Jon Voight turning tricks, Dustin Hoffman pounding on the hood of a car in *Midnight Cowboy*.

My high school friends and I used to cut classes and go to Times Square Records, underground, accessible only through the subway station. We'd flip through stacks of 45s to find obscure songs by singers and groups we liked, the Marvelettes, Barbara Lewis, Lee Andrews and the Hearts. We thought the porn theaters—showing films like *Thigh Spy* and *Undercover Lovers*—were hilarious. It all seemed so vibrant and colorful, so raw and grown-up and alive. Before the advertising codes kicked in, vodka poured endlessly from a bottle into a perpetually empty glass, and the Camel cigarettes sign puffed like an awakening volcano.

People came from everywhere, a cross section of everyone checking out everyone else, watching from shadowy doorways, propping open the doors to dark halls and darker staircases that led up to . . . what? This was before the intersections swarmed with furry animals accosting terrified children and pressuring their parents into taking photos. The delicious smells of smoke and meat wafted from the hot dog stands and the $1.99 steak house. People dressed up to come here, in wide collars, platform shoes, bell-bottoms, shiny polyester shirts, fashions that made everyone look as if their wrists and ankles had outgrown their clothing.

Tony's press conference was being held in one of the seamy low-rise hotels in the West 40s that rented rooms by the hour. Let's call this one the Savoy. Most of the guests were hookers and their clients. Lately these hotels had started renting out party spaces, also by the hour, for modestly budgeted conferences and lectures. The attendees were the first alien emissaries from Planet Times Square Gentrification.

At the Savoy, a tall young woman in lilac hot pants and a lime green wig was leaning on the reception desk and gossiping with the desk clerk, who waved me around the corner toward the conference room.

I was late, on purpose. I hadn't wanted to wait around, with Tony, for people to show up. But Ellen had said that she was going to be there and that quite a few reporters had signed on.

The conference room was a smallish space, redone for low-cost weddings and retirement parties, for motivational speakers working up to fancier venues. The walls were covered with flocked paper, red on red, like the wallpaper at Ernie's, where Scottie first sees Madeleine Elster, except that the Savoy's wallpaper was chipped, with patches of white showing through. The carpet was also red, but a bloodier scarlet, flecked with grayish polka dots and what looked like animal hair. The room smelled like Tony's building in San Francisco.

The chairs were faux gilded, delicate. Party chairs more suitable for a princess-themed birthday party than a political press conference.

Around thirty white men in short-sleeve shirts and ties perched, visibly uncomfortable, scattered over rows of fragile chairs, talking quietly to their fellow reporters. I slid into a seat on the aisle, three-quarters of the way back. I passed Ellen, who was sitting in the last row on the aisle, but I didn't say hello, and I was glad she didn't see me. Up front there was a camera, lights, a guy with earphones and a boom mike.

Tony was already at the microphone. Had anyone introduced him? He wore a light tan suit, a white shirt and striped tie, the outfit he'd worn in some of the photos taken outside the Los Angeles courthouse. He'd gotten a haircut since last night. Maybe his lawyer or Ellen had taken him to a barber early this morning. I hoped so. It would mean that someone was keeping an eye on what was going to happen.

Tony looked the way I remembered him looking in San Francisco: thoughtful, preoccupied, haunted maybe, but not paranoid, tormented, or manic. The jacket and tie were a good choice. I was relieved. Maybe what happened yesterday was an unfortunate reaction to a pill he'd taken for the flight. It happened. People snapped. They landed in the ER, and in no time they were as good as new. In college, I'd visited friends in the psychiatric unit, and days later they were back in class.

Tony tapped the microphone. The room got quiet.

He said, "I see some old friends here, but for those of you who don't know me, I'm Anthony Russo. I'm the guy who talked Daniel Ellsberg into leaking the Pentagon Papers."

A few people applauded. Tony dipped his head and smiled.

"As most of you know, I'm free to stand before you today only because a team of sleazy incompetent criminals broke into Dan Ellsberg's psychiatrist's office."

There was some laughter but also a subsonic hum of unease. They knew how the Pentagon Papers trial ended, overshadowed by the bigger break-in. As a target for a top secret mission, the Democratic headquarters had made an LA shrink's office look like a joke. I gripped the edge of my seat until its tracery dug into my palms. If I could just relax my hands, the rest of me would follow. It occurred to me that it was what I told myself in the dentist's chair.

Tony said, "I'm here today because part of the documents wasn't widely circulated. No one seems to have paid attention. I myself was unaware of it until recently, when I opened those seven thousand pages at random, pages for which Henry Kissinger thought we should be executed. I was shocked—as you will be—by what neither Ellsberg nor Kissinger nor the *New York Times* nor I myself noticed at the time."

Tony lifted a box of paper from under the lectern and began to walk slowly down the aisle, distributing packets: two pages stapled together, printed on both sides. He greeted some of the men by name and seemed not to recognize others. His head was slightly lowered, and there was a doggedness, a restrained ferocity, in how he handed out the papers—part Caliban, part Jehovah's Witness, part crazy schoolteacher.

Paper. This was when it was still common for strangers on the street to press photocopied pages into your hands, handwritten narratives spelled out in letters scissored from newspapers, descriptions of bruising encounters with the psychiatric establishment, visits to other galaxies, complaints about being monitored by the KGB. Those rambling diatribes were the last thing I wanted to think about as I waited for Tony to work his way to me, which meant that I couldn't think about anything else.

Tony nodded but barely seemed to see me. He gave me the stapled papers and the reflexive smile he gave the reporters whose names he'd forgotten. He blinked and moved on. I felt a pressure behind my eyes, threatening to spill into tears. Only the reporters mattered now. Tony was here to talk to *them*. I was a girl he drove around and slept with, in San Francisco.

But he had asked me to be here.

I told myself, He's trying to salvage something from the wreckage. I told myself, This is about something larger than your confused little romance with Tony.

Watching him among those men, I understood the obvious thing that I hadn't realized in San Francisco. Even if he seemed perfectly sane, which he didn't, it would be hard for him to get a job. He'd been in jail. Probably he couldn't work for the government, not even at the city or state level. The companies that could have used his skills would see him as a massive security risk. Corporations were not exactly lining up to hire a whistleblower. Maybe he could get that part-time gig at a progressive radio station. He needed to write the book that would be his path to redemption, the book currently stuffed into a carton in his agent's office. Those nights in San Francisco, we'd floated over the city like figures in a bubble in a painting by Bosch. To see his true situation, I'd had to be surrounded by ambassadors from the world from which he'd been exiled, visitors from a locked room that might never readmit him.

I overheard a man near me say, "What *is* this, Frank?"

Frank said, "Fucked if I know."

I flipped from the first to the second page and back. There was some text from the Pentagon Papers. Something about Lyndon Johnson. A blurry diagram with arrows, like a treasure map. It wasn't clear what the arrows meant. There were some labels—place-names, I assumed—in Vietnamese.

"This was the epicenter of the bombing in 1967. Ground zero. 1–9–6–7!" Tony spelled out the numbers.

By now the reporters were side-eyeing one another and discreetly shaking their heads.

One raised his hand. "Respectfully, Tony, can you explain to us what's new here?"

"The extent of the damage," said Tony. "The year it happened."

A guy behind me asked his friend, "Is this nuts, or am I imagining that this is nuts? Everyone knows about this."

His friend said, "Honestly? Honestly? I honestly don't *know* what this *is*. I can't read it."

After a while the boom mike was lowered, the camera shut off. The crew slipped away. Also discreetly, but still. Only the house lights stayed on.

Tony said, "These maps are central to the history of the war. Our crime—*one* of our war crimes—is that dark splotch in the center of the map. If we look at that stain, if we really *see* that stain, if we are willing to admit our mistakes and take responsibility for that stain, for what we know, for what we knew then, for what we allowed to happen, only then will we see the truth and begin to wash the blood from our hands.

"That dark spot is what we did to the Vietnamese people."

I looked at my map. Then I looked over the shoulders of the men on either side of me, all looking at the pages. I looked at *their* maps.

There was no dark spot on anyone's map.

I was among the first to leave the room, crouched half over, as if exiting quickly and awkwardly would make me invisible and keep Tony from seeing me go. Maybe he didn't see me. Maybe he saw me and didn't care.

I don't know why I ran, why a surge of panic overrode my loyalty and undermined every idea I had about friendship and responsibility. I don't know how a rush of adrenaline disarmed my conscience and compassion, how it blotted out the memory of the months I'd spent with a person I cared about, maybe even loved, and who was going mad in public. I'd wanted Tony's courage and idealism to rub off on me, but all I seemed to have gotten was his guilt, his fear and regret.

I thought of things he'd said before, and I saw them in a new way. I thought of the rambling, the tears, the driving. I remembered his story about speaking at a gala dinner with Dan and ranting on past midnight.

I stood in the seedy lobby, sweating, leaning against a wall that also seemed to be sweating, a chilly drip from a struggling vent. I couldn't go back into the conference room. Maybe I could make up an excuse for why I'd left. A coughing fit. I needed the bathroom. Sorry. I hope it wasn't distracting. Except that I couldn't do it. My body would have rebelled. I didn't want to go back in.

Maybe it bothered me that so many of our conversations had been about him, that so much of our attention had been focused on him. But who else would it have been about? He was a famous antiwar hero. I was a young woman who wrote novels. Maybe it bothered me that the reporters were the only ones who seemed to matter to Tony. But that made sense as well. Maybe the voice in his head was saying: You still have a chance to stop the war. Or else you can forget about that and have an intimate chat with a girl whom you drove around in your car and whom you had less-than-ecstatic sex with. It occurred to me that I'd been starstruck by a star that was burning out even as I watched.

It was wrong to blame Tony for something that wasn't his fault. He had seen so much, done so much, been so brave, wagered so much and lost. I should have stayed to make sure that someone was looking after him. I knew that then. I know it now. But I didn't stay. I ran.

Charles Dickens created an army of villains, from the lawyer Tulkinghorn to the criminal Bill Sikes, from the violent convict Compeyson to the schoolmaster Gradgrind. But the one who scares me most is a mid-level offender, *Bleak House*'s Mrs. Jellyby, with her concern for the starving children in Africa and her disregard for her own kids, who get their heads stuck in the stair rails and barely avoid disaster. "Telescopic philanthropy" is Dickens's harsh diagnosis, and it haunts me still: wanting to make the world a better place and ditching a friend in trouble. Nor does it comfort me to realize that Dickens *was* Mrs. Jellyby, raising money to help fallen women, widows, and orphans while often showing a wounding disregard for his own wife and children.

When he handed me the photocopied pages, Tony hardly saw me. Maybe I was more hurt and annoyed by his coolness than I wanted to admit. I wasn't brave or committed or unselfish enough. I lacked the virtues and strengths that would have made me go back into the conference room. Instead I ran out of the Savoy hotel as if the building was about to explode.

It's hard to remember being so easily thrown off-balance. It's hard to remember that tentativeness, that fragility, a luxury that family and work have made impossible to enjoy. It's hard to remember feeling as if my psyche were one of those eggs that high school students are assigned to carry around, presumably to teach them what it's like to care for a newborn, presumably to lower the teen-pregnancy rate, even though an egg doesn't cry all night and is nothing like a baby. It's hard to remember my fear that a few bad choices meant that I was doomed forever, that nothing was ever going to change.

It wasn't love. If it were love, I would have stayed. If it were love, I would have moved to the front row and let Tony know that I was there. It wasn't love. I told myself that Ellen and Tony's lawyers had been with him at critical moments, in dicey situations. They understood his history. They would know what to do. If I offered to help, the lawyers wouldn't even know who I was. I'm a friend from San Francisco. We used to drive around in his car.

I walked out into the awakening hive of Times Square. The pimps and dealers were chatting, getting ready for work. Hot dogs were twirling in the grease, the deep fryers were starting to sizzle, giant pretzels were browning and puffing up around the snowy flakes of salt. Young guys stood around, alone and in groups, smoking and staring into the middle distance. There were fewer cars, but the traffic sped by. The signage shouted, Ties! Cigars! Pizza! Fun! Triple XXX! Girls Girls Girls! The marquees were lighting up. *Thigh Spy. Lecher. The Devil in Miss Jones. In Person XXX.*

It was a gorgeous spring morning. On the corner, a woman in a flowered babushka was selling bunches of bright yellow daffodils in metal pails glistening with water.

I felt unsteady. Faces popped at me like flashbulbs. A zombie army had arisen from under the sidewalk. I moved through crowds of grinning mutants bred to survive on carbon monoxide. I needed to get a grip. I needed to be careful. This was not the ideal time and place to feel as if I were high on acid.

The press conference had been painful, destabilizing. So had the scene in Ellen's office and the dinner in the loft. It was confusing to find that sadness, disappointment, and relief could coexist at such high concentrations.

I felt at once lighter and heavier, more divided and more whole, as if some missing part of myself had returned after a long absence. I felt justified. I felt young. I felt free. I felt like a monster who would never be forgiven.

I never saw Tony again.

During the days that followed the night that Tony came to dinner, only one of my Soho roommates asked what had happened to him. I told her that he was having a hard time and that he'd gone back to California. I don't know why I assumed that.

I called Henry, who said that Tony had been MIA for a while. Henry had thought that maybe he'd gone home to Virginia, but actually Tony was back in San Francisco. They'd spoken briefly on the phone, but Henry hadn't seen him.

I tried Tony's number in San Francisco. I held my breath while his phone rang. I forgot what I was planning to say. I wasn't surprised when he didn't answer.

I moved out of the Soho loft and went to stay with some friends who were renting a farmhouse near New Haven. I'd known some of them since high school. They were kind and easygoing. I needed to get out of the city.

My friends in the farmhouse were teachers, carpenters, graduate students. Late in the afternoon we sat in the living room of the dilapidated comfortable house, on the dilapidated comfortable couches, and watched the final installment of the Watergate hearings and Nixon's resignation.

My friends felt purely clean and joyous about justice being done, but I still felt uneasy because I had left Tony to fall apart in front of people he hoped would bring out the book he was never going to write. I didn't talk about him to anyone at the house, and they had no reason to ask.

Regret shadowed those bright days of triumph and dimmed the happy voices of my friends. Watching the hearings, I wondered what Tony would have said. He was one of the earliest beneficiaries of the Watergate break-in, even if he believed that the scandal had made the world forget the point of the sacrifices he'd made.

Later that summer I was invited to be a fellow at the Bread Loaf Writers' Conference. The Green Mountains of Vermont were beautiful. My meals were cooked, my room pleasant enough. I met people who became lifelong friends.

I was fortunate, I knew. I should have felt happy and honored to be there, but something set me against it. I loved hearing the poets read, but some of the older fiction faculty were writers I didn't much admire, and when they drank, from before lunch on, some of the men got predatory with the female students, or, as they were called, contributors.

I was uneasy with the complex hierarchy, with the solemn procession of sycophants queueing to praise the conference director after his endless poetry readings, and especially with the big unspoken lie about the contributors' chances of being published if they listened to the advice they got in conference with the established writers.

I set up shop on the porch of the pretty frame house where I was staying and which bordered the main campus walkway. I charged five dollars for a tarot reading.

I had never read for strangers before. I was surprised that I was good at it, but maybe I shouldn't have been so amazed.

Maybe this too was part of being a writer, intuiting things about people from their responses to certain images, certain words.

I began to schedule appointments. The conference director asked me to stop. He said I was being disruptive. He said that people were getting their fortunes told when they should have been going to workshops and readings. He implied that unless I quit the bogus fortune-telling I would not be invited back the following summer. I said it wasn't *fortune-telling*, but offering an alternate way of seeing the world. He said that was a technicality.

I said, "All these people paid eight hundred dollars for one opinion, why shouldn't they pay five dollars for another?" I was sorry the moment I said it, but there was no going back.

I kept on giving card readings until the demand ran out and I got tired and a scary guy who looked like Charlie Manson asked me to read his cards. People told me that they'd never seen him before, that he wasn't part of the conference.

I made $500 reading tarot that summer, money I needed. Bread Loaf wasn't paying me except with the scenery, the room and board, and the honor of being there.

I wasn't invited back for the next few years, and then I was asked again. I taught there for many summers in a row, partly because so many of my dear friends went there, and later because I was, essentially, getting paid to bring my sons to a two-week summer camp in Vermont.

Now this seems like a story about how you can be an ill-mannered and ungrateful guest while convincing yourself that you are being a stealth warrior for truth and transparency. But it's also a story about being young and inflexible, convinced that the truth is an absolute, that every lie, however harmless and small and kindly meant, is a crime against humanity.

If the '70s was about the discovery that the ideas and arti-facts of the preceding decade could be monetized, wasn't that what I was doing, reading cards for money, telling writers what they'd come to Vermont to hear for a modest fee of five dollars?

For years after that, I traveled to San Francisco, on book tours and for readings and such, but I never lived there again. It no longer reminds me of *Vertigo*. The low-rise glass-and-steel condos look just like everywhere else, and the land-marked Victorians look like Disneyland.

I heard that Tony went back to Virginia after his house on the beach in Santa Monica was destroyed by a hurricane. I heard that he traveled back and forth to California, and that near the end of his life, he was considering running for office on the Peace and Freedom Party ticket.

Henry and Grace moved up the coast, and I rarely saw them. Once, after a bookstore reading in Marin County, a man came up to me and asked me to sign his book.

I said, "I know you from somewhere."

He said, "We used to be married."

It was my first husband.

I said, "I'm so sorry. I'm not good with faces." Everything I said made it worse.

Henry was there. He and my former husband had become good friends again, as they had been in high school. After the signing, Henry and my ex-husband invited me back to Henry and Grace's house in Marin. Grace was off somewhere with their daughter.

We drank tea in the pretty backyard, which looked a lot like the garden behind the Parnassus Street apartment. Henry had a gift for gardening, I realized only then. I must have thought that our yard in San Francisco took care of itself. Henry and my ex-husband invited me to go for a hike up Mount Tamalpais, but I was wearing high heels, and I have never been much of a hiker.

Another year, I was having lunch at Tadich Grill, on California Street, when I got a phone call informing me that my mother was dying in New York. It changed my feelings about San Francisco forever.

I've gone back to the city, but it just seems melancholy now. I think about my mother. I think about walking to North Beach with Emmet, about riding around with Tony, and it makes me sad. I leave as soon as I can. Once, maybe twice, I've detoured past the house on Parnassus Street. I've stood in front of it, trying to persuade myself that I lived there, that I was ever that young.

Tony died in 2008, of heart disease, in Virginia. When I heard about his death, my first thought was: All that stress, all those cigarettes, and he ate so badly. I never knew what changed in his life and what didn't. I hope he found someone to love.

That he never once tried to contact me after we last saw each other meant something. And what did it mean that, in all that time, I never once tried to find out where he was? We lost track of each other, and we let ourselves forget.

The Most Dangerous Man in America features footage of Tony, taken later in life. He'd obviously recovered his balance since the last time I saw him. On film, he looks and sounds just like he did when I knew him in San Francisco—appealing, charming, good-humored, only older. He looks older than his years, and he seems to be having a little trouble breathing.

Available on YouTube, a webinar panel marking the fiftieth anniversary of the release of the Pentagon Papers begins with the clip of Tony in a garden talking about Prisoner AG132, saying what I heard him say on Moira's editing machine and at the Martha Washington—the same stresses, the same tears welling up at the same points, the same head shake at his inability not to be *moved* by the memory of the conversation that changed him forever.

It's strange, sitting at my desk, staring at my laptop, at Tony, who in the film appears to be around the age that he was when I knew him. He's sweeter-looking and more handsome than I remember. His hands are delicate and beautiful. His smile is warm, appealing, and his charm is turned on in full force. It is, as he would have said, very moving.

Why had I found the exact repetition—the performative aspect of his stories—so troubling? By now, I have learned that Tony was right: You find the best way to tell a story, and that's how you tell it. By now, I've told certain stories often enough to understand why someone might fall back on a well-rehearsed version of a life-changing event.

Hearing Tony recite the Vietnamese prisoner's poem on film makes me wish he'd written his book. Choosing his interview with Prisoner AG132 as the tipping point was not only the truth; it was also a literary decision. He knew what novelists know: that humans are drawn to, *moved by*, characters who aren't ideas masquerading as human beings. AG132 was a person. He had a life, a vocation, a song, a poem he loved. His song moved Tony, and Tony believed that it would move anyone who heard it.

During the fiftieth-anniversary Zoom panel, the historian Barbara Myers says that the story about Prisoner AG132 was Tony's way of giving the Vietnamese a human face. She is remarkably clear about who Tony was and what he stood for: He wanted us to know that AG132 wasn't the enemy; that the prisoner was a teacher, a person who had led a difficult and dangerous life and who cheered himself up with a poem. He wanted us to know that AG132 was more like us than our soldiers were told, more like us than we were encouraged to think about the guerrilla fighters emerging from tunnels and creeping through the jungle onto our TV screens.

In the film, Tony says, "Several of the interviews were very moving. And one interview in particular, I look back now as being a real turning point in my life, actually. He recited a poem for me. It was very moving, very moving to hear him recite this poem right in the middle of this interrogation room in a jail where I knew people had been tortured, if not killed. And he sang a song for me. And when he sang, he threw his head back and he sang in a very proud way. It was one of the most moving things that ever happened to me."

"The Other Conspirator," Barbara Myers's sympathetic and incisive film about Tony, ends with a scene in a wood-paneled, softly lit interior. Daniel Ellsberg is speaking from the pulpit at Tony's memorial service in 2008, talking about Tony's meeting with Prisoner AG132.

Ellsberg says, "Every time I heard Tony mention this man, he would always . . . Tears would come to his eyes, and he would break down at the meaning this song had for him."

Talking about his old friend, Ellsberg switches into the present tense.

"Tony says, 'Could you give us a sample of the poems you like best?'

"Answer: 'The following is the poem that I like best. I recite it whenever I feel downhearted'—"

Ellsberg breaks off. He clears his throat and, on the edge of tears, he puts his hand to his heart.

He says, "I'm channeling Tony here."

It's a powerful moment. I think we would feel its intensity even if we knew nothing about what happened between the two men. In *The Most Dangerous Man in America*, Ellsberg speaks of reconciling with Tony not long before his death, but says nothing about when or how this occurred.

Daniel Ellsberg is channeling Tony channeling Prisoner AG132. It must be a challenge, becoming the conduit for a ghost, almost like being a medium, without saying that's what you are.

Ellsberg-as-Tony says, "I recite it whenever I feel down-hearted and it never fails to cheer me up.

"War cease. Peace reappear.

"*Let . . .*" Ellsberg stops. "Can I get some water?

"Let the millions of young trees sprout their leaves and stretch their limbs.
Let the barren land turn into bountiful farmland.
Let the poisoned crop return to life again.
War cease the deadly game.
Let the frightening slaughter vanish.
Let the farmers walk their contented feet to the paddy field.
Let the paddy ears drink ecstatically the milk of the dew.
War cease. Let the prisons open their gates.
Let the sweet hands gentle the young hair."

The film switches to Tony, who says the next lines without a break, as if he is continuing to recite the poem that Ellsberg has begun:

"Let the people live in peace and abundance.
Let the fresh smile blossom on the young lips.
Let the war cease on the Ben Hai River.
Let the millions of hearts—"

Tony breaks down. He keeps going.

"Let the millions of hearts know the joy—"

He cries again. He shakes his head with a quick self-conscious laugh. He can't say *hearts*. He can't say *joy*.

"Let the millions of hearts enjoy the joy of reunion.
Let everybody visit all our Fatherland."

The film cuts back to Ellsberg, who now seems barely able
to speak for the emotion shaking his voice.

"Let everybody visit all of our Fatherland.
Let the North and South enjoy the day of reunification."

Vertigo can make us ask ourselves, if only for the length
of the film, if a spirit can come back from the dead and possess
the body of the living. For a moment, we enter into Scottie's
obsession, and almost believe, as he does, that Judy may be the
red-haired reincarnation of Madeleine.

If Ellsberg—speaking from the chapel pulpit—is imitating
Tony, he doesn't seem to know it. He believes he is *becoming* his
old ally. He jokes that he is *channeling Tony*, letting his friend
speak through him as they recite the poem that changed Tony's
life.

By the fiftieth anniversary of the release of the Pentagon
Papers, Tony had been dead for thirteen years, but when the
webinar producers wanted to capture the drama of that historical moment, they included the footage of Ellsberg and Tony
reciting the prisoner's poem. Perhaps it seemed like the most
heartfelt and *moving* narrative associated with the release of the
Pentagon Papers, not a story about a secret caper carried out at
great risk, not a story about a Xerox machine or a Los Angeles courtroom, but a story about the moment when an enemy
revealed his true nature as a human being. Perhaps the story
of Prisoner AG132 was simply a better story than any of the
events that changed Ellsberg's mind.

One winter I attended a crowded camp meeting in a community of spiritualists in Central Florida. A medium in a filmy blue gown prayed for heavenly guidance and delivered messages from the beyond to her congregation. I watched a woman in the audience weep when she heard that her dog was being taken good care of. A man was relieved to learn that his uncle had forgiven him for never coming to visit.

I found it hard to sit through the service. I couldn't tell what the medium believed or what she thought she was doing. The version of me who had spent her twenties casting the I Ching and reading the tarot had grown more skeptical and pragmatic. I was no longer the person flirting with the occult, wanting to think that the most improbable things were the most likely. Yet there was no way not to feel the yearning—the longing—in the air in the spiritualist chapel. As far as I could tell, everyone there believed what the medium was saying.

Why was Ellsberg "channeling" Tony? To steal his story, to make it his own? Maybe it was love. Maybe he was recalling a moment of hope and glory, untarnished by what happened later. Maybe he was mourning the past, those hushed office conversations, those nights when he and Tony were Butch Cassidy and the Sundance Kid, true to themselves, outlaws breaking laws that had to be broken, doing something important and brave. Or maybe he was weeping because of the end of his friendship with Tony, because of Tony's misfortunes. Maybe he was channeling a time when he and Tony thought they were changing history, saving lives. Or maybe he was mourning his own youth, which can happen when we remember the dead we loved when we were young.

In an unpublished transcript of a conversation between Tony and Peter Davis, who was then gathering material and footage for his Oscar-winning film, *Hearts and Minds,* Tony circles back to the story of Prisoner AG132.

What Tony kept trying to say was that his respect for Prisoner AG132 and his hope that Prisoner AG132 wouldn't hold him accountable for the bombing of Vietnam, combined with Tony's *own* guilt and fear that he *was* accountable, came together in a moment of startling clarity: the moment when you actually *see* another human being. Tony fell in love with Prisoner AG132, the way you can fall in love with someone you know for a day or a week and never touch and never see again.

Do I miss Tony? Often, when something happens in the wider world, I wonder what he would have said about it. I miss him when I see a young woman who is the age I was then, and I remember how easy it was to fall under a charismatic older person's spell. I remember him when I try to love the girl I was then, at once so uncertain and so sure of herself, so terrified and so brave, so close to the beginning of everything. I think about Tony when I hear people talking about the crises we face now, saying that they feel helpless, that there's nothing that can be done. I think about how Tony believed that you had to do *something.* At least you had to try. That's what we believed at that time: You couldn't let things just happen. Even if you couldn't do much, even if the chances were that most of what you did would eventually be undone, you still had to try.

I've searched folders and files full of old papers, but I've never found the letters I got from Tony between my leaving

San Francisco and his arrival in New York. I did find other letters that I didn't remember receiving.

Among them are letters from two different boyfriends, both of them writing to ask if we had broken up and they hadn't noticed. Apparently I'd disappeared.

I knew I'd done something like that to Tony and to my first husband, and later to a musician I lived with in Virginia and left to go to New York without mentioning that I was never coming back. I hadn't realized that it was a pattern. I was shocked that I had been ghosting people before *ghosting* became a word, before email and texting made it easier and more common. I'd wanted to believe that I was always a thoughtful, kindhearted, responsible person. One danger of writing about yourself is that you may learn things about yourself that you don't want to know.

Something about those letters made me rethink our pursuit of so-called sexual freedom, how much of it was an excuse to treat other people as if they didn't fully exist. It revived my Mrs. Jellyby fears. I'd wanted to stop a war in Asia, but I had ignored whatever unhappiness I'd caused men who had done nothing to deserve it.

I was young. The young are ruthless and desperate because they don't know what they want and don't know how to get it but know that they need to find it, sooner rather than later. Despite what the old say about the young, the young know that they won't be young forever.

I tell myself that not everyone is born with a conscience, that our moral sense can develop at any age. We can change. We can change our minds. Sometimes, when people have asked what my novels are "about," I've said, for want of a better answer, or *any* answer at all, that some of them are "about" how a person develops a moral conscience, or not. Maybe the subject interests me because I feel that my own conscience developed a little late.

I am no longer the young person who could leave her friend to go mad in a sleazy hotel ballroom. But I have sympathy for her. I tell myself that when I left Tony at the Savoy that day, I was following the marching orders of my future. If I still believed in destiny, I might think that I had no choice.

I've lost count of how many times I've seen *Vertigo* since then. Each time the film seemed to be saying something different, and I began to understand that it was saying many things. I stopped thinking that the film was solely about the absurd demands that men make on women, the obsessive fetishization of our hair, our clothes and shoes. I understood that it is about how obsession is so contagious that Scottie catches a serious case of the fixation that Madeleine is faking. I understood that it is about how love can loosen our grip on reality and forever skew our understanding of the order of the world. I understood that it is about the mystery of death, about how we see the dead walk past us on the street, how there is no word for what Scottie feels when he keeps seeing the dead Madeleine in women who, up close, look nothing like her.

I understood that the film is about time's refusal to reverse itself, to go backward to the moment before grief began. I understood that it is about the dead's refusal to return and give us a second chance to fix what we got wrong, to do and say what we withheld when they were alive. I understood that the film is saying: We don't always *get* a second chance, though Scottie is still demanding one, in the film's final scene. I understood that the film is about how you can kill someone with the power of your fears, your fixations and inconsolable sorrows. I understood that the film is about San Francisco, about how the camera can't resist those sweeping panoramas over the city, can't withstand the temptation to look over the characters' shoulders at the view from their windows.

The last time I saw the film was five years ago. It was being shown at Bard College, in the auditorium of the magnificent Fisher Center. Projected on a big screen, the film was accompanied by a full orchestra, the violins pouring everything they had into the overheated, brilliant Bernard Herrmann score.

I decided to take my granddaughters: Emilia, who was ten at the time, and Malena, who was six. I'm not sure why. I thought that seeing the film with a live orchestra might be a once-in-a-lifetime opportunity. I thought (correctly, it turned out) that the girls wouldn't be bored. I thought that they would be able to follow the plot. Maybe I had the crazy idea that Hitchcock was an antidote to the poison of Disney princess culture, though if there was ever a princess, it was Kim Novak's Madeleine Elster. I knew they would understand that the blond princess is really Judy in a tailored gray princess costume.

When the string section began that frantic jittering and those dizzying swoops, before any images appeared on-screen, Malena put her fingers in her ears and said she wasn't going to be able to stand it. The film was too scary. It was a testament to the power of Herrmann's score, to its mystery, its threatening melancholy and dread. Malena thought of herself as a toughie. Several times we'd had to talk her out of watching the slasher films she'd seen with friends and claimed to enjoy. I whispered that she'd be okay, that there was no gore in *Vertigo*, no blood. And she was. She was fine. She liked it.

In the second half of the film, during the scene in which Scottie first sees Madeleine in Judy and wants to believe that he hasn't lost the woman he loves, that she has come back from the dead, I was startled when Malena asked me what was wrong. Why was I crying?

I hadn't realized I was crying. I couldn't answer. I didn't know. I'd been thinking about how much of the film is about driving around San Francisco.

"I guess the movie's sad," I said.

"Duh," Malena said. Then she added sweetly, "Don't cry," to make sure that I knew she loved me.

I think that was when I realized that at some point I would write about San Francisco, about 1974, about that year when so much changed, that year when the city looked like it did in *Vertigo*, even though it didn't. I think it was then that I knew I would try to describe those nights when the neon striped Tony's windshield, when the neighborhoods seemed haunted, when the bay seemed deep and dark, the bridge dangerously high, the time when Patty Hearst and her captors blackened the windows of their safe house, when Herrmann's score soared and pulsed beneath the Delfonics. *If you don't know me by now.*

I think I knew then that someday I would write about another time when another war was being fought on a distant continent, in the past that keeps returning like a recurring dream, a time so different, so almost unimaginable, so unlike the present moment that the best I can do is write: Maybe that was who I was. Maybe this is what happened.

ACKNOWLEDGMENTS

I've changed the names of everyone except for public figures. The events and conversations I've included happened. I've recorded what people told me, regardless of whether I knew if what they were saying was true. Any attempt to recall dialogue verbatim will be approximate, at best, but I have tried to capture the voices of the people I knew and to describe what they did and said. The epigraph from Saint Teresa is a paraphrase.

Many thanks to Judy Linn, who heard the story and first suggested that I write this. I'd like to thank the filmmaker Peter Davis for his extraordinary generosity in sending me the transcript of a long interview with Tony Russo that he ultimately decided not to include in his Oscar-winning documentary, *Hearts and Minds.* The historian and filmmaker Barbara Myers kindly shared her keen insights into who Tony was. Her film, "The Other Conspirator," provided invaluable help. Thank you to my first readers: Leon Michels, Scott Spencer, Jo Ann Beard, Michael Cunningham, Doon Arbus, Neal Selkirk, Karen Sullivan. I'm grateful to Howard Rheingold, Judy Maas, Roger Rosenblatt, Marshall Smith, Monroe Engel, William Alfred, Harry Ford, and Freude Bartlett. Thank you, Denise Shannon, Sarah Stein, Sara Nelson, Jonathan Burnham, and always, always, Howie Michels.

FRANCINE PROSE is the author of twenty-two works of fiction, including the highly acclaimed *Mister Monkey*; the *New York Times* bestseller *Lovers at the Chameleon Club, Paris 1932*; *A Changed Man*, which won the Dayton Literary Peace Prize; and *Blue Angel*, which was a finalist for the National Book Award. Her works of nonfiction include the highly praised *Anne Frank: The Book, The Life, The Afterlife* and the *New York Times* bestseller *Reading Like a Writer*, which has become a classic. The recipient of numerous grants and honors, including a Guggenheim and a Fulbright, a Director's Fellow at the Center for Scholars and Writers at the New York Public Library, Prose is a former president of PEN American Center, and a member of the American Academy of Arts and Letters and the American Academy of Arts and Sciences. She is a Distinguished Writer in Residence at Bard College.